"Do not train a child to learn by force or harshness; but direct them to it by what amuses their minds."
- Plato

"Life without knowledge is death in disguise."
- Talib Kweli

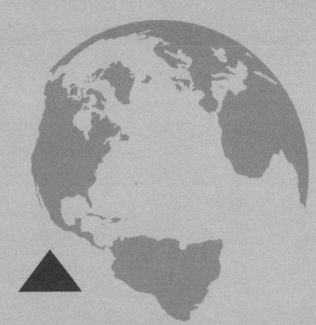

Flocabulary Presents

Hip-Hop History of the World Part I

THE FLOCABULARY ARTIST TEAM

AKIR, PLAY, NETTY, REASON, RIDDICK, ESCHER, GREY, TRAJIK, 9TH WONDER, ALEX, SPECTAC, DILLON

ISBN: 1-934773-11-5
13-Digit ISBN: 978-1-934773-11-6

Writing and Research by Andy Vietze
Editing and Proofreading by Blake Harrison, Laura Sicilino-Rosen and Marty Keiser
Lyrics and Performances by Escher, Dillon Maurer, J Bully, Spectac, Trajik, Netty, Baba Brinkman, Alex Rappaport, Grey, Reason and Ben Hameen
Music by Alex Rappaport, Batsauce, Ed Boyer, Jay Lifton, Shadowville, XO Music and Sean Divine
Cover Design by Bashan Aquart
Layout by Danielle Thomas

Books by Flocabulary are available in digital formats and at special discounts for bulk purchases by educational institutions and programs. Address inquiries to:

Flocabulary
315 W. 39th St.
Suite 1610
New York, NY 10018

Or visit us online at:
www.flocabulary.com

Printed in India

TABLE OF CONTENTS

WHAT IS HISTORY?

The history that we study in school is really just a tiny glimpse of what's happened in the past. We have to make choices about what to study and what to ignore because we could never possibly learn about the actions of all the billions of people who have lived and died on this planet. Just think about yourself: Will you be studied in history books when you're old or dead? You might be. But you probably won't.

The history that we study is the history of those people and events that have shaped thousands of lives and have led to the world that we currently live in. In this book and on this CD, you will hear some of the most amazing true stories ever told: The rise and fall of powerful empires, the alleged adventures of wild and mighty gods, the actions of people who have created things that have revolutionized the world, and the brave (and maybe foolish) battles fought by men and women again and again.

You may feel like the people in these pages don't seem like you. In many ways, they weren't like you at all. Up until very recently, most people thought that it was totally cool for a powerful army to go kill people and take their land. Throughout history, most people only cared about their own groups: people who looked like them or lived in the same place or had the same religion. For all the people who looked different: They killed them or made them pay taxes or made them slaves. History is full of ugly facts like this. Unfortunately, some people still live this way.

But in many other ways, the people in these pages *are* like you. Humans are humans. As kids they played, as teens they fell in love, as adults they struggled to raise their own kids. They laughed at jokes. They danced to music. If they hit their head on a tree branch, their friends would make fun of them. There are some things that don't change from century to century. There are some things that do. Which way are we headed now? It's up to us. It's up to you.

THE
SONGS

CHAPTER 1:
WE'RE NOMADIC

Hunter Gatherers: 7 Million BC to 2000 BC

Cave Paintings

INTRO

Early humans couldn't read books, but they could read something else: tracks. When your food is always moving, you'd better learn how to find it. So early humans were trackers. They were extremely talented at analyzing hoofprints, broken blades of tall grass, and the smell of animal droppings. It was a tough life, but they were good at it. But one of history's lessons is that nothing stays the same forever. People changed, the climate changed, and new technologies led to incredible shifts in how people lived. Probably the most remarkable change of all didn't come with the invention of the airplane or the light bulb or even the wheel. It came with the invention of farming.

WE'RE NOMADIC

LYRICS

*Alright, so what you're saying is if
I put this in the ground and then I
put some water on it, something is
going to grow? Ahh, you sure?*

Man, we didn't always look like this,
We didn't have fire,
Couldn't cook like this.
We didn't sleep with a pillow,
Lived in trees originally, so if you
Cried you would weep in a willow.
But one monkey comes down;
It's cool,
When he gets up on his hind legs,
He can use tools.
Might kill a bird or two, but that's
Not happening much,
Instead, he's picking blueberries
And he's gathering nuts.
But what's this?
He's making a stone knife,
Now he's hunting antelope his
Whole life.
But it's a cold night;
With no light it's dark as cocoa,
No home –
That could drive a sane man loco.
Picture this like Kodak:
He roams, he's a nomad,
Following herds of pachyderms
Wherever they go now.
He rubs two sticks, makes a fire,
Now his meat and food
Is so easy to chew.
This African man was
Mostly grunting,
Couldn't think in our terms,
He didn't have words.

CONTEXT AND BACKGROUND

Man, we didn't always look like this...

Where did humans come from? This question has been asked by thousands of different societies throughout history, and each one came up with an answer. Australian Aborigines believed that humans were the children of two gods: the morning star and the moon. The Greeks believed that humans were made out of clay by the god Prometheus. More recently, however, scientists have found evidence that points to a different idea.

Bones found buried in the ground provide strong evidence that humans evolved from other **great apes**. Humans' closest living relative is the chimpanzee. In fact, 98.4% of human DNA is identical to that of a chimpanzee. That means that humans and chimps have more in common than rats and mice.

But one monkey comes down, it's cool...

Scientists call modern-day humans **Homo sapiens** (Latin for "wise man"). We have evolved over millions of years from other great apes, including Homo ergaster ("working man"), Homo habilis ("handy man"), and Homo erectus ("upright man"). These were men and women who walked upright and used tools but had brains smaller than ours are now. They were **hunters and gatherers**, and they began the process of **migration** — moving around the Earth. Homo sapiens, too, would cover a lot of ground. The earliest modern humans date back 200,000 years to Africa. By 11000 BC, they occupied every continent except Antarctica.

He gets up on his hind legs, he can use tools...

Humans are not the only species to use tools. Some chimps in Africa use spears to hunt, and gorillas have been seen using a long stick to figure out how deep a river is before jumping in. What made humans and their ancestors so good at using tools was their upright posture. Walking on two legs meant their hands were free to grip a spear or knife.

Picture this like Kodak: he roams, he's a nomad...

For much of human history, for millions and millions of years, up until just 11,000 years ago, people hunted for their food, following animals. Their lives revolved around the seasons and the habits of the animals they hunted. When bison herds were on the move, for example, people were right behind them. Their homes were movable shelters like tepees. Their possessions could all be carried. They set up camp, hunted, and were ready to follow the animals when the animals left.

Makes a fire, now his meat and food is so easy to chew...

Research suggests that the earliest controlled use of fire by hominids dates from about 1.4 million years ago. These people couldn't *make* fire; they'd just take fire from where lightning struck and then try to keep the flames going. Not until about 7000 BC did humans acquire reliable fire-making techniques, using friction or flint. Meat that was cooked was easier to chew and digest, and so much tastier.

FLOCAB SPITS FACTS LIKE AN ALMANAC

Lions have sharp claws and teeth. Antelope are amazingly fast sprinters. Elephants are insanely strong. We humans are fairly slow (even giraffes and pet cats can run faster). We're not the strongest, and we lack sharp teeth and claws. So how could humans compete with other animals and hunt them? Two reasons: We are great at using **tools**, and we have amazing **endurance**.

Because we stand upright and have opposable thumbs, using tools is easy for humans. But we are also amazing at running long distances. Because we sweat, we are able to keep our bodies cool much better than other animals can. Dogs, antelopes, cats, and many other mammals don't sweat, but pant to stay cool. This means that they easily overheat. So humans could chase an antelope for hours and hours (sometimes even days) and wait for the beast to overheat. Then humans could make an easy kill. It's sweat that makes us best.

LYRICS continued

So he makes a word for fire,
A word for water,
A word for his son and his daughter.
He does another thing
That no animal tries,
He paints paintings on the cave
Wall; why?
I don't know but he's an African,
He's an Ethiopian,
And guess what kid, so are you...
Because he made babies,
And they made babies,
And they made babies,
And they made a baby
And that baby is you!

Oh, we ain't got no homes,
So all we gonna do is roam.
We're not Romans,
But we're roaming,
We're nomadic,
So you know we keep it going.

OK,
I don't even need a hand at all,
I will bury the dead
Like a Neanderthal.
I'm Cool Herc meets Kirk,
Your flow captain,
I throw spears like a Cro-Magnon.
That's the early man,
He was going insane,
Tired of chasing animals
Across the plains.
His wife's picking berries
And fruit from the trees,
She's like, "We could grow food if
We plant these seeds."
Now she's like,
"This is sweet, my man,
We eating bread from the wheat

Couldn't think in our terms, he didn't have words...

The world we understand is determined by how our brains make sense of the things we see, hear, feel and remember. Words take this to a whole new awesome level, and they also serve a very practical purpose: communication. Let's say I killed a bear, and I wanted to tell the rest of my tribe where it was. Without words, I would have to take them there myself or draw a picture. But with words, I could say, "Hang a left at the old tree," and then go take a nap. Words made communicating so easy!

He paints paintings on the cave wall, why...

In the 1940s in France, four teenage boys stumbled into a cave. There they found walls and walls covered with art – more than 600 paintings of animals in all. It turned out that those illustrations in **Lascaux, France**, were more than 15,000 years old. Early peoples were not only hunters but artists. Art was important to them. They painted walls and made sculptures of bone and rock. Cave paintings have been found in many cultures throughout the world. Why did they paint? What do you think?

I will bury the dead like a Neanderthal...

Neanderthals were another type of early hominid. Some scientists believe that they were the first species to bury their dead. So when your brother died, instead of just leaving his body where the vultures can get him, you could bury him. This places an increased importance on life.

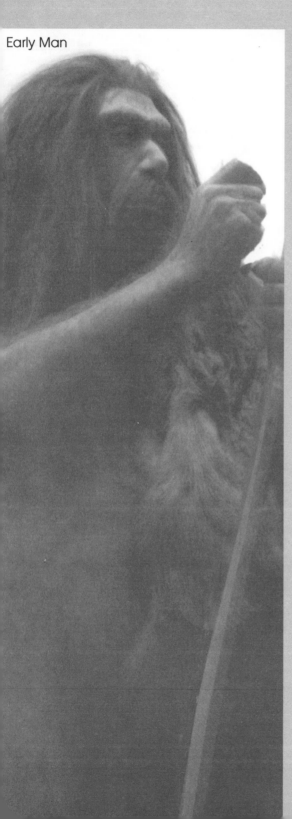

Early Man

I throw spears like a Cro-Magnon...

Cro-Magnons, another type of people, appeared in Europe 35,000 years ago. They made some great tools and pioneered spear-throwing, which made them much better hunters than the Neanderthal. Cro-Magnons looked very similar to people today, and they probably merged with the rest of Homo Sapiens unlike the Neanderthal, who disappeared.

She's like, we could grow food if we plant these seeds...

While the men were out hunting, the women often gathered nuts, berries and grains, and took care of the kids. At a certain point, some women (and some men) may have realized that they could make food grow by planting seeds. This was an earth-changing discovery, and it happened in societies all across the globe around 8000 BC. At that time, nomadic hunters made the switch to domesticated life.

We eating bread from the wheat we plant...

The era of hunting with sticks and chasing animals around is called the Stone Age. When people settled down and started to farm, the New Stone Age began. It was a big change. Historians call it the **Neolithic Revolution.**

Those animals you hunt, let's domesticate them...

At some point, as people made the change from hunting to gathering, they began to keep animals in pens. Someone must have thought, "It sure

LYRICS continued

We plant.
Those animals you hunt,
Let's domesticate them,
Put a fence around,
Now we're baking bacon."
We ira-irrigate, control water flows,
Plow the land, plant the crops,
And watch them grow.
Now my brother doesn't even
Have to farm no more,
The Bronze Age – he's making
Bronze arms and swords.
Division of labor, that's the plan,
Now my aunt can go and open
That frozen yogurt stand.
You better know, we trade it like
Joe's, and settle down,
Like Jericho, kid,
We built the cities and towns.
You better recognize.

Hook

would be easier to kill these animals if we could just put a wall around them, then we wouldn't have to walk all over the place to get our food." Sheep and goats were likely the first animals that people had a domesticated-type relationship with, sometime around 9000 BC. There was a transitionary time, though, because sheep herding was somewhat nomadic, too; people had to follow the animals around to find the best grass. Cows and pigs were probably the next **domesticated animals,** around 7000 BC. Cows changed everything because they provided milk as well as meat. And cattle could also be used as muscle in the fields. They were big and strong and could drag plows, making life easier on the farmer. Farming began to look like a nice option for a lot of people.

We ira-irrigate, control water flows...

Most of the earliest villages grew up around water sources. This is true all across the globe because humans need water to survive and water made farming much easier. The Mesopotamians had the Tigris and the Euphrates. The Egyptians had the Nile. The rivers gave farmers more than just water to **irrigate** their plants with. It also provided soil that was fertile and ready to grow things. Irrigation was the catalyst of civilization. It began a series of changes that would lead to cities and eventually the modern world.

Farmers settled alongside rivers. Then they built villages. Then they decided to work together to best use all the water. They dug canals and moved the water around to irrigate all of the fields, which led to great growing conditions and, soon,

13

FLOCAB SPITS FACTS LIKE AN ALMANAC

Word Numbers
Humans use 200 muscles when they say "hi."
An ape can learn 1,000 signs to communicate with.
There are 6,000 languages spoken around the world today.

When did people use dogs as pets? At some point, thousands and thousands of years ago, man realized that wild dogs could help him locate other animals to hunt. By feeding the dogs some of the food, the dogs would stay loyal to him, barking when dangerous animals approached and helping him hunt. More recently, humans have brought dogs into the home, almost like a furry little friend.

Why do people kiss? Kissing came from a strange place. Early humans would chew food for their young children (who couldn't chew meat) and then pass the food to their kids mouth-to-mouth. At some point, this affectionate gesture from mother to daughter or son was tried without food, and it became a hit.

surpluses of food.

Now my brother doesn't even have to farm no more...
Once there was more than enough food to go around, it became clear that not everybody needed to be a farmer anymore. The **specialization of labor** occurred. Some people became artisans or crafters – they made things. These new items could then be traded. Trade was one of the impetuses for written language, which, in turn, helped spread technologies. And so on. Another consequence of canal digging was that people had to figure out whose job it was to look after the canals. This is what led to early forms of government.

Historians define **civilization** as a society in which people have the following: permanent homes; farms for food growing; written language; some form of government; and specialization of labor.

The Bronze Age, he's making bronze arms and swords...
At some point, prehistoric people learned how to heat metals to create spear-tips and knives. Early on, people figured out that combining copper and tin together made an extremely strong metal called bronze. This began an era known as the **Bronze Age,** which started around 3000 BC.

Like Jericho, kid, we built the cities and towns...
The switch from hunting to farming happened all over the world. It's uncanny how it occurred in so many different places simultaneously without people being able to talk about it. It happened in Africa, the Middle East, and Mesoamerica, for example

– regions that didn't know the other existed. The first known place for it to happen was **Jericho**, in what is now Israel. Jericho is the oldest known town with a real population — 2,000 people. And they lived primarily on what they grew, as opposed to what they shot. Another great village was found at **Skara Brae** in the Orkney Islands of Scotland. During the 1850s, a huge storm revealed a series of stone buildings. Archaeologists discovered that the settlement dated back to between 3200 and 2200 BC, the late Neolithic period.

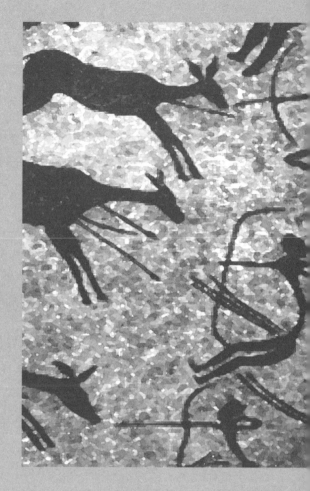

HISTORY SPEAKS

"Doubt is the father of invention."
– Galileo Galilei

"Courage is the first of human qualities because it is the quality which guarantees the others."
– Aristotle

CHAPTER 2:

WE'RE IN THAT FERTILE CRESCENT

Fertile Crescent Civilizations: 3000 BC to 500 BC

Sargon II

INTRO

Welcome to the birthplace of civilization. That's what many historians consider the **Fertile Crescent**, a large chunk of land between the Persian Gulf and the Mediterranean. Surrounded by desert and irrigated by two mighty rivers, the **Tigris and the Euphrates**, the Fertile Crescent occupies the region we now know as **Iraq and Iran**. These two rivers snake down the mountains of the north and drain into the Persian Gulf. They frequently overflowed their banks, leaving behind a rich soil that was ideal for growing crops. As is always the case, it was water that allowed powerful civilizations to grow.

WE'RE IN THAT FERTILE CRESCENT

LYRICS

A Sumerian:
We're chilling like it's summer,
In our Sumerian city-states,
Inventing the arch,
We put it on our city gates.
We built the temples, ziggurats,
We're swimming when it's very hot,
In the Tigris and Euphrates, baby.
In the Tigris and Euphrates, baby.
In the Tigris and Euphrates, baby.
Each city is unique,
We don't have to wear a uniform,
But when we're writing it,
We write it in cuneiform.

Sargon:
I roll through, invading them;
I'm Sargon the Great,
Empire builder for the Akkadians.

Hammurabi:
Sorry Sargon,
Your empire couldn't last,
I babble on these tracks,
Put Babylon on the maps.
I'm Hammurabi,
You can call me Papi,
Made a strict code,
'Cause your laws were sloppy.
Hammurabi's Code matches
Tooth for tooth,
Poke an eye out
And get yours poked out too.

An Assyrian:
We're the Assyrians, assassins,
Seriously dangerous
When we're blasting,

CONTEXT AND BACKGROUND

We're chilling like it's summer, in our Sumerian city-states...
On the Persian Gulf end of Mesopotamia was a region called **Sumer** where farmers built villages that grew and grew, just like the grains being planted. These early settlers built homes using bricks made from the mud the Tigris and Euphrates left behind, and by about 3000 BC there were enough houses to make small cities. Farmers worked together to create irrigation and drainage ditches to direct water where they wanted it and help prevent the great rivers from flooding the cities.

By this time, many city-states had grown in the Fertile Crescent: Babylon, Ur, Uruk, Eridu. **City-states** were just as they sound — cities so large and independent that they became much like states are today, governed by a single ruler and each with their own justice system, trade and military.

Inventing the arch, we put it on our city gates...
The Sumerians are credited with some of the most amazing inventions in human history. They invented the **arch**. They made wagons, the first-ever **wheeled vehicles** (the wheel itself was probably invented earlier). They accurately tracked the stars. And they decided to divide time into blocks of 60: They put **60 seconds in a minute**, and 60 minutes in an hour.

We built the temples, ziggurats...
Sumerians were a **polytheistic** people

FLOCAB SPITS FACTS LIKE AN ALMANAC

Problem #1
Walls are preventing my armies from entering a city to conquer it.

Solution
Dig under the walls to make them crumble, and use battering rams, large logs carried by several soldiers to ram and destroy gates and doors.

Inventors
The Assyrians

Problem #2
Bronze is expensive to make. It requires copper and tin, and I can't find much of either one.

Solution
Use iron instead. It's nearly as strong, and much easier to produce. Soon this will start the Iron Age, during which almost all weapons and armor will be made from iron.

Inventors
The Hittites, the Chinese

— they believed there was not just one but many gods, whose favor they needed to live good lives. Each city-state had a particular favorite or patron god. In honor of these deities, the people built huge temples, like pyramids with stairs up the sides. These were **ziggurats**, and they were often the centerpieces of city-states.

But when we're writing it, we write it in cuneiform...
The Mesopotamians used etchings on stone tablets to tell their stories and display their rules. They developed some of the earliest forms of writing. The system used by Sumerian scribes was called **cuneiform**, and it used small geometrical shapes scratched into wet stone that later dried and hardened to recount stories and keep track of trade, taxes, military issues, and more. Thanks to the widespread use of cuneiform, historians know much about Mesopotamian culture and the many transformations it went through over the centuries.

I'm Sargon the Great, empire builder for the Akkadians...
Sargon is thought to be the first ruler in world history to have a permanent, standing army at his command, an army that was one of the first to use bows and arrows. He was the emperor of the **Akkadians** around 2000 BC. Sargon used his troops to create the world's **earliest empire**, a huge territory in the Middle East. For the times, it was a vast kingdom; the world had never seen anything like it.

I babble on these tracks, put Babylon on the maps...
Impressive as it was, Sargon's empire didn't last. All empires were (and

WE'RE IN THAT FERTILE CRESCENT

LYRICS continued

We took your men captive.
Burnt Babylon,
Built a library instead,
With that old book:
Epic of Gilgamesh.

What?
We're in that Fertile Crescent,
Sargon, you smell,
Need some Herbal Essence.
I keep it quick,
Like a turtle's breakfast,
Time's up,
Better learn your lessons.

Nebuchadnezzar:
Nobody ruled better,
I'm Nebuchadnezzar,
Me and my Chaldeans
Are sharper than cheddar.
We're so holy like Swiss cheese,
One day my wife said,
"Neb, I miss trees.
This city life is too hard for me,
All is see is brown, baby,
I need garden-green."
So I built the Hanging Gardens of
Babylon for my girl,
It's one of the seven wonders
Of the world.

A Phoenician:
Phoenicians:
Where we get our alphabet from.
Phoenicians:
Trading, and standing strong.
Phoenicians: We set sail on seas,
Built ships with ease,
Sail from Sidon to Sicily.
The best craftsmen,

still are) based on power, which is based on the threat of violence: Whoever has the strongest army will rule. The **Babylonians** were the next power-hungry army to conquer Mesopotamia.

I'm Hammurabi, you can call me Papi...
The Babylonian army was led by a mighty leader named **Hammurabi** (1792-1750 BC). He rose to power much like his predecessor Sargon, driving wedges between the cities of Sumer and systematically conquering each one in turn. He had a well-trained army of ax- and spear-toting foot soldiers.

Hammurabi's Code matches tooth for tooth...
Mesopotamia became famous for what was long thought of as the first written code of laws in the world. (Historians now say there were earlier codified laws.) These laws were brought into being by Hammurabi. **Hammurabi's Code**, etched into a tablet, included 282 laws based largely on the principle of retribution: If you poke out a free person's eye, your eye is poked out, too. It meted out harsh punishments for crimes, especially when they were committed by people of the lower class. Mesopotamian society was strongly divided by class. and it gave men far more rights than women.

We're the Assyrians, assassins...
In about 700 BC the **Assyrians,** a people who lived in the hills at the end of the Tigris River, moved into the area that Hammurabi had ruled. Using iron

19

weapons (like the Hittites to the north), they soon acquired all of the Fertile Crescent and much of the surrounding territory. They did this the way most conquering happens: by killing people. Luckily for their enemies, the Assyrian empire lasted less than a century.

With that old book: Epic of Gilgamesh...

When your army enters a city, you, as general, had three basic choices: You could occupy this, take everything valuable and leave it, or burn it to the ground.

When the Assyrians invaded **Babylon**, they chose option number 3. But all wasn't lost. One of the great things they did was build a royal library, which housed a copy of one of the oldest stories ever written down: the Epic of Gilgamesh. **The Epic of Gilgamesh** is a long poem about a legendary king named Gilgamesh who may or may not have existed. Regardless, the epic tale written down most certainly contained some myths (made-up stories) as well.

Nobody ruled better, I'm Nebuchadnezzar...

The Assyrians were toppled in part by the **Chaldeans**, who came from present-day Syria. It was their **King Nebuchadnezzar** (605-562 BC) who was the next great ruler of the area. He rebuilt Babylon, making it once again the most important city in the region. The Greek historian Herodotus described it as having walls 56 miles long and 320 feet high (though archaeological evidence has them at about 10 miles long and not nearly as high). According to the Bible, the city-center was dominated by the enormous Tower of Babel.

LYRICS continued

We make the best crafts,
We blow the most glass,
We make the most cash.
Trade the glass and crafts,
Watch our paper stack,
Dye cloth, people like,
"I gots to have that."

Hook

A Hebrew:
You don't have to barter,
Lydians made cents,
'Cause Lydians printed coins
Like a mint.
Between Egypt and Babylon,
We're the Hebrews,
Tribes and crews;
Today we'd be called Jews.
Wandering the desert,
Avoiding bandits,
Till Moses showed us
Ten Commandments.
Divided into 12 tribes, we got lost,
Until King Saul finally reunited us.
Next, David built Jerusalem,
In the Bible, he defeats Goliath,
Ya heard of him?
His son Solomon built the temple,
We weren't saved,
Chaldeans invaded
And made us slaves.

Hook

So I built the Hanging Gardens of Babylon, for my girl…
It was the **Hanging Gardens of Babylon** that became one of the seven wonders of the ancient world. Legend has it that they were built to please Nebuchadnezzar's wife, who missed the green, mountainous land that she came from. So her husband had a terraced garden, overflowing with plants, constructed for her. By all accounts it was extraordinary – from a distance the greenery seemed suspended in air. Unfortunately, it was destroyed by earthquakes around 200 BC.

Phoenicians: Where we get our alphabet from…
Along the Mediterranean coast of the Middle East, a unique civilization was doing things a little differently. They were the **Phoenicians**. One of their legacies is our modern-day **alphabet**. Their alphabet was adapted by the Greeks and then the Romans; it's not too different from the one we use today.

Phoenicians: Trading, and standing strong…
The Phoenicians realized that power wasn't just about having the biggest army; it was also about having the most money. So they built a **trading empire** that connected various tribes and civilizations around the Mediterranean. But what's the best way to get goods from one place to another? Not on rickety old carts where bandits can rob you at every turn, but on fast ships.

Phoenicians: We set sail on seas...

The Phoenicians built a lot of impressive ships. Their ships made it all the way to Britain and the west coast of Africa, bringing wood, slaves, and glass to the Greeks and North Africans.

Dye cloth, people like, I gots to have that...

The Phoenicians invented glassblowing, but the truly hot product everyone just had to have was **purple dye**. They got the dye from a special kind of sea snail that basically sneezed it out. Only the Phoenicians lived near the snails, so only they had the royal purple dye. Apparently, it was so expensive, it was worth its weight in silver. In fact, the word *Phoenician* means "purple people" in Greek.

You don't have to barter, Lydians made cents...

In nearby Turkey in 687 BC, the **Lydians** rose to power. Their king was Gyges, who was friendly with the Greeks (who were gaining power to their west). The Lydians wrote themselves into history by issuing the **first gold coins**. Before then, no government had ever come up with its own single currency.

Between Egypt and Babylon, we're the Hebrews...

Meanwhile, on the Mediterranean coast in a place known as **Canaan**, the **Hebrews** were organizing a state under a series of kings. The Jews differed from other cultures in the region because they were **monotheistic** — they worshipped a single god, known as Yahweh – and they were nomadic, following their herds.

Till Moses showed us 10 commandments...

According to the Bible, the Hebrews weren't always monotheistic. At one point they worshipped many different deities. That changed when Moses brought the Ten Commandments down from a mountain, and the Hebrews agreed to worship only one god.

Until King Saul finally re-united us...

In the mid-1000s BC, **King Saul** united them, getting all the tribes together to face the Philistines, who lived on the same seacoast. This began a battle that still continues to this day in the Israeli-Arab conflict in Middle East.

Next David built Jerusalem...

After Saul, **King David** defeated the Philistines and other enemies and conquered the city of **Jerusalem**, which he made his capital.

His son Solomon built the temple...

In about 965 BC, King Solomon, David's son, came to power.. **King Solomon** made Hebrew control over the area complete. He built an empire for his people and, according to the Bible, the First Temple in Jerusalem.Solomon, David's son. **King Solomon** made their control over the area complete and he built an empire for his people. According to the Bible, he built the First Temple in Jerusalem.

Lil' Baby Moses

HISTORY SPEAKS

"If you lie and then tell the truth, the truth will be considered a lie."

– Sumerian Proverb

"When man wanted to make a machine that would walk, he created the wheel, which does not look like a leg."

– Guillaume Apollinaire

CHAPTER 3:

HAMMURABI'S CODE & ROME'S TWELVE TABLES

INTERLUDE

1760 BC & 450 BC

LYRICS

Hammurabi's Code.

"If a man put out the eye of another man, his eye shall be put out.

If he break another man's bone, his bone shall be broken.

If a man knock out the teeth of his equal, his teeth shall be knocked out.

If he put out the eye of a man's slave, or break the bone of a man's slave, he shall pay one-half of the slave's value."

CONTEXT AND BACKGROUND

Hammurabi's Code was not the first set of laws to be created or written. Archaeologists have found Sumerian laws that are 300 years older, and even those aren't believed to be the first ever. But Hammurabi's Code is famous for a few reasons.

First of all, the laws themselves are brief and amazingly strict. Hammurabi probably didn't invent the idea of **retribution** (something making up for something else), but his laws show retribution at its purest form.

Secondly, the laws themselves are beautifully presented. The entire code was etched into a single, giant stone, eight feet of polished black basalt. At the top of the statue are two figures: the king of Babylon (Hammurabi himself) bowing before one of the gods. Below that, the 282 laws that form the code were etched in cuneiform. The statue stood in a public place in Babylon so that all the people could know what laws governed them. Sounds pretty fair, right? The tricky part was that hardly anyone could read.

Rome's Twelve Tables.

"A dreadfully deformed child shall be killed.

Our ancestors saw fit that females, by reason of lightness of mind and of disposition, shall remain in guardianship, even when they have become adults.

No person shall hold meetings in the City at night.

If any person has sung or composed against another person a song such as was causing slander or insult...he shall be clubbed to death."

Rome's Twelve Tables are a set of ancient laws that stood at the foundation of Roman law, and formed the basis of the constitution of the **Roman Republic** (509 – 44 BC). Originally the Roman Republic's laws were kept secret, which allowed people of the upper class to punish a plebeian (member of the lower-class) for almost anything. Several plebeians finally convinced the Republic's leaders that laws should be written down for all to see. So they created the Twelve Tables.

The Twelve Tables were a lot like the Bill of Rights in America. They didn't list all of the laws or rights that a person had; they just listed some of the major ones. The laws were strict and included some extremely harsh penalties, but at least they were finally written down. And many scholars believe the council who wrote the laws did another favor for the people of Rome: They wrote the laws so that they rhymed. This helped the Roman people remember the laws. Scholars aren't positive about this, however, because the original tables themselves were destroyed during an invasion of Rome. What survives are brief excerpts quoted by other authors.

Take a look at the laws in this chapter. Which do you think make sense? Why do you think each one was written?

Hammurabi's Code

CHAPTER 4:
WALK LIKE AN EGYPTIAN

Ancient Egypt: 3200 BC to 1000 BC

INTRO

While the people of the Fertile Crescent were farming and fighting, a strange, beautiful civilization grew from the rich soil along the **Nile River**. These were the **Egyptians**, whose unique customs and impressive architecture have always attracted our special attention. Take, for example, the role of the cat in ancient Egypt.

Egyptians were the first people to domesticate the cat around 2000 BC. From then on, cats were considered types of gods on earth. Egyptian hunters took cats on their hunts instead of dogs. According to one source, the Egyptian army once surrendered a battle because their enemy released cats onto the battlefield and the Egyptians didn't want to hurt them. Have you ever seen a mummy, a dead person wrapped in cloth so their body would be preserved? Well, the Egyptians even mummified their cats. In one temple, scientists found more than 300,000 dead cats wrapped up in cloth. The ancient Egyptians were truly a one-of-a-kind people.

WALK LIKE AN EGYPTIAN

LYRICS

They say that the Nile
Gave us Egypt,
Try planting crops on the beach,
And you can believe it.
The yearly flood left rich dirt
Called silt,
So they planted in the silt
And the farms got built.
Around the Nile, they got together
To feel alright like Bob Marley,
Planting cotton, wheat and barley.
Writing on papyrus in hieroglyphics,
That's the Egyptian alphabet
You can get with.
"Am I a dimwit? I can't believe it,
I can't read it,
Looks like symbols to me,"
Naw, it's simple you see:
The Rosetta stone let us know
How to decipher the code,
So now we study the old words
That were written in stone.
They believed in an afterlife,
They'd get strips of cloth and
They'd wrap you tight.
Yep, pharaohs
Would get mummified,
And buried with food and clothes
For the great unknown, whoa.

Walk-walk like an Egyptian,
Walk-walk like an Egyptian.
We built the pyramids,
We built the Sphinx,
And then we wrote it down
In hieroglyphics.

CONTEXT AND BACKGROUND

They say that the Nile gave us Egypt...
Perhaps no other nation owes more to a river than Egypt. The Nile made life in this dry desert possible. In fact, the entire country is sometimes called "the gift of the Nile." The Nile River Valley is practically rainless — without the river there would be no water; without water, there would be no life. The river starts far south of Egypt in the highlands of Africa where rains fall and snows melt. It flows north for 4,000 miles all the way to the Mediterranean Sea, bringing life with it. Because the river flows north, the "Upper Nile" is actually to the south, while the "Lower Nile" is to the north.

Each year the Nile floods in a very predictable way. Farmers figured this out early, and were able to use the river to irrigate their crops. The river was also used for travel, and most of Egyptian life took place along it. It was so important to the early civilization that all of ancient Egypt's cities were built at its side. Actually, the vast majority of the population of modern Egypt still lives right along the banks of the Nile today.

Try planting crops on the beach, and you can believe it...
To water their crops, the Egyptians dug canals on both sides of the river to move the water where they wanted it. They also built basins to capture floodwaters when the river was high. Egyptian farmers were responsible for moving the water around by carrying it in big jars to fields farther away from the river. In the 16th century BC, the

shadouf was introduced. This was a beam that sat on a post – on one end was a water scoop, on the other a weight. The farmer could dip the scoop into the river or canal, swing the arm out over a field, and let the water drain where he wanted it. Shadoufs made moving water a lot easier.

The yearly flood left rich dirt called silt...

Silt was the rich, fertile soil that the Nile left behind after it flooded. It allowed early Egyptians to grow crops on the land, instead of having to roam around with their animals. The farming of the land led to the development of villages, towns, cities, and eventually one of the greatest civilizations the ancient world had ever seen. All because of some extra-special dirt.

Writing on papyrus in hieroglyphics...

The Egyptians were some of the first people to ever write anything down. They used a system of symbols to communicate as early as 3300 BC. There were as many as 2,000 symbols; each one represented an idea, object, or even a sound. These **hieroglyphics** were sometimes very artistic, and were usually carved into stone. Some scribes made paper from the papyrus reeds they found on the banks of the Nile. They laid the reeds down and pounded them into paper, which was lighter and easier to transport than rocks. This new writing paper took the name of the reeds and was called **papyrus**.

The Rosetta stone let us know how to decipher the code...

For thousands of years after the end of the ancient Egyptian civilization, people appreciated how pretty hieroglyphics were, but couldn't read them. All the information in the hieroglyphics was lost. This all changed in 1799, in a town called Rosetta, in Egypt, when archaeologists found the **Rosetta stone**. This smooth dark stone is almost four feet tall, and it has three different languages written on it. Because the same passage is written in Greek, demotic (another ancient language) and hieroglyphics, historians have been able to figure out the meaning of many hieroglyphic symbols. The stone effectively translated the language of ancient Egypt into words that historians could understand.

They believed in an afterlife...

Egyptians believed very strongly in an afterlife. We know from their "Book of the Dead" that after death, a person's soul travels to the hall of the dead. There, the dead person's heart is said to be weighed against a "feather of truth." If the heart weighed less than the feather, then it was considered a good heart. The person's soul was taken to Osiris, god of the afterlife. If the heart was heavy, though, it was said that a person was evil. That heart would be eaten by a demon that was part crocodile, part lion and part hippopotamus.

Pharaohs would get mummified...

The **pharaohs** (or kings) of ancient Egypt had it pretty good. They were considered gods on earth and could basically do whatever they wanted. Like lots of people, they were anxious about what happened to them after they died. They wanted to bring their favorite things with them, and they believed that in order for their soul to exist in an afterlife, their bodies must

LYRICS continued

Osiris:
I'm Osiris, lord of the dead,
Don't mess with me, boy,
I'll put a sword to your head.
We fight invaders effortlessly,
'Cause we're insulated
By the desert and the seas.
Upper and Lower,
We're divided up,
Yep, until Pharaoh Menes.
He united us.
In 3100 BC, he said,
I want my son to be pharaoh
After me, I'll start a dynasty.
King Tut died before he got old,
But King Tut got a mask
Made of gold.
So pharaohs sit back,
Sip tea, and get rich,
While workers break their backs
To build the pyramids.
Fifty stories tall, that's incredible,
They used ramps to move stones,
So they're handicap accessible?
If you were pharaoh
Whose last breath goes,
You got buried in a pyramid,
Like it's your gravestone.

Hook

Isis:
Let me ask you a question:
Who's the nicest?
"You!"…That's right, I'm Isis.
I'm what people believed
Before Allah or Jesus,
Without me,
Osiris would still be in pieces.
I'll spit it like a camel;
I'm on that flow tip,

be preserved. Thus **mummification** was invented.

You've seen the movies about mummies walking around all wrapped up in rags? The Egyptians really did wrap their dead to make sure that the body didn't decay. They removed the internal organs and placed them in specially decorated urns called **canopic jars,** dried the body with special salts and oils, and wrapped it with linens. And they did a good job of it: Some mummies were still whole when archaeologists opened their tombs 2,000 years later.

I'm Osiris, lord of the dead...
Osiris was the god of death, life and fertility in ancient Egyptian religion, now known as Egyptian mythology.

We fight invaders effortlessly...
You know the old real estate saying "location, location, location?" The Egyptians had it. Besides the Nile, which gave them life-giving water, the people had the Mediterranean Sea to the north with its fish and cool breezes. The Nile and the Mediterranean did something else, too: They protected the kingdom of Egypt from invasion. The Nile waterfalls of Upper Egypt were hard to sail down, so the south was covered, and the Mediterranean made the approach of armies to the north very predictable. The deserts to the east and west were too hot to move troops through quickly. So the Egyptians were able to go about their business in relative peace, something not many other cultures could do.

Until Pharaoh Menes united us...
The cultures of Upper and Lower Egypt differed slightly; they had their own dialects, patron goddesses and

FLOCAB SPITS FACTS LIKE AN ALMANAC

The sound you hear at the end of the song comes from King Tut's trumpet. Yes, King Tut's actual trumpet. But it's not King Tut who is playing it.

While unearthing King Tut's tomb in 1922, archaeologists found a lot of cool stuff that belonged to King Tut: the first-ever sofa bed, 30 boomerangs used for hunting, and two beautiful trumpets. One trumpet was silver, the other was copper. Both were decorated with beautiful carvings.

In 1939, someone decided they wanted to try playing it. BBC radio was there to record the beautiful ancient sound. The trumpet, which hadn't been played in more than 3,000 years, let out a few graceful notes. Then it shattered. Oops!

crowns. King Menes united them in 3100 BC.

I'll start a dynasty...

In ancient Egypt, the pharaohs were king. These were the guys for whom the pyramids were built. You've probably seen the giant masks they were buried with. How could you not have a big head when everyone thought you were a god on earth? The first pharaoh historians know about was **Menes**, who ruled around 3100 BC and is known for uniting all of the Egyptians communities. He built his capital at Memphis — the one on the Nile, not the one in Tennessee. (He also founded a gator-sounding city called Crocodopolis.) And he set things up so that his family would be in power for a long time to come: He started a **dynasty**.

King Tut died before he got old...

King Tut is probably the only Egyptian whose name is known to almost everyone in America. As pharaohs go, **Tutankhamen** (c. 1370-1352 BC) wasn't much of one. He took the throne when he was still a boy of nine, and he died at the age of 18. He owes his legacy to British Egyptologist Howard Carter, who dug up his tomb in 1922. It was full of amazing gold and artifacts because it hadn't been looted the way so many Egyptian tombs had. Inside was a wealth of treasures and a lot of information about ancient Egyptian life. One of the men who opened King Tut's tomb with Carter died shortly thereafter, giving birth to the "curse of the mummy" that's been made into many movies since.

LYRICS continued

Tell ya'll the story of Amenhotep.
The Pharaoh who wanted
Egypt to go worship one god,
Instead of several.
I'm one of lots of gods: polytheism,
He thought there was just one:
That's monotheism,
And that that one god
Was the Sun god,
And that he, as pharaoh,
Was the son of the Sun god.
He renamed himself Akhenaton,
He kicked all the priests out,
And that shocked 'em.
But when he was deceased:
Pay back,
The priests and all their gods,
They came back.

Hook

So Pharoahs sit back, sip tea, and get rich...
If you want to talk about great pharaohs, Ramses (II) is the name to remember. There were a lot of Ramses but only one **Ramses the Great** (c. 1279-1212 BC). He came to power not long after Tutankhamen and began to rebuild the Egyptian empire that had been lost under some of his predecessors. His reign was noted for the sheer number of buildings he had constructed — more than any other pharaoh. Ramses' most famous structure was at Abu Simbel in the south of the country. It featured four massive statues of... guess who? Ramses himself, as tall as a skyscraper. He was so revered by his successors that 10 other pharaohs took his name. It was under Ramses II that Egypt enjoyed the apex of its power. He had quite the harem and was said to have fathered more than 100 children. His mummy, like King Tut's, was found well preserved.

There were not very many female pharaohs; of them, **Hatshepsut** (1473-1458 BC) was the longest ruling of all. She was the favorite child of her father, Pharaoh Thutmose I. When her two brothers died, she was the next in line, though there had never been a queen pharaoh before her. She was popular and beautiful, and her father had been a beloved pharaoh, so the people listened when she took the throne. Even so, she faced many difficulties being a woman in a traditionally male role. Women at the time, however, enjoyed more rights in Egypt than they did elsewhere. They could buy property and were considered equal to men before the law. Hatshepsut was a savvy political operator; she knew that the people would respond better to her if she looked the part of a pharaoh. So she dressed as kings had before her, and even wore a ceremonial beard. Hatshepsut was able to get quite a lot done during her 15-year reign — she built more temples and statuary than any other Egyptian queen.

While workers break their backs to build the pyramids...

We all know the Egyptians were fond of pyramids. But they also had a society that became known as the **social pyramid**. It was built on a class structure, which can be thought of as a pyramid in shape. Your place in this hierarchy depended on your place in society. At the top, of course, was the pharaoh. Underneath him was his vizier, or head of priests. Below the vizier were the high priests and the nobles. Below them was a sort of middle class of government officials, priests, doctors and engineers. Next were the writers and artisans. And finally, spread across the base, were the farmers and the slaves. Much of this stratification was based upon birth, but some people did move up the pyramid via their skills and occupation.

Most people think of the pyramids when they think of Egypt. The biggest pyramid of all belonged to **King Khufu** (2585-2560 BC), whom the Greeks called Cheops. Khufu ordered the **Great Pyramid of Giza** built. He apparently wanted to make a statement with his last resting place. It covered 13 acres and rose almost 500 feet up into the air — about as tall as a 50-story building. More than 2 million limestone blocks were used to construct this monument; each of them weighed more than a large pickup truck! The sides of the gigantic tomb were so tightly constructed that not even the thin blade of a knife could be slid between the blocks. Of course, he didn't break a sweat during the process, but had thousands of workers do it for him. By most accounts he was a tyrant obsessed with the construction of his great pyramid. He seized property to pay for it and even sold his own daughter into prostitution.

Fifty stories tall, that's incredible...

As you can imagine from the sheer size of them, building the pyramids was a monumental effort. These gigantic gravestones were marvels of early architecture and engineering. In the city of Cairo alone there were 67 of them. Ancient Egyptians didn't have huge trucks, cranes, and earthmovers, of course. They had to do all of the work with manpower alone. Many people assume that slaves did all the heavy lifting, but that wasn't always the case – historians now believe the Great Pyramid of Giza was built using freemen. Modern scholars think it took about 20,000 people 20 years to complete Khufu's tomb. And he was supposedly not very nice and in a hurry to get it done.

To build the pyramids, workers in quarries cut chunks of limestone, alabaster, granite, and basalt rock. These were squared off and taken to the pyramid's site. There, **ramps** were run up to each level to allow workers to haul blocks ever upward, often with the help of oxen. Scholars today believe that it was the ramps that enabled rocks weighing more than 10 tons in some case, to be lifted up (others have theorized that Egyptians used pulleys or levers).

You got buried in a Pyramid, like it's your gravestone…
The pyramids were built not as apartments for the living, but as amazingly large **tombs** for the dead. But not all pharaohs were wrapped up and put in pyramids.

The great **Valley of the Kings** is the burial ground of many pharaohs from the New Kingdom. For more than 500 years, from the 16th to the 11th centuries BC, the kings of Egypt built their tombs in the Valley of the Kings. Known as the home of both King Tut's and Ramses' mummies, these tombs were built into rocky cliffs.

I'm Isis. I'm what people believed before Allah or Jesus…
Isis is the Egyptian goddess of magic, healing, beer, bread and green fields.

Without me, Osiris would still be in pieces…
According to Egyptian mythology, Isis had two brothers: Osiris and Set. Set got jealous of Osiris one day and so he hacked him into little pieces. Isis (who was also Osiris's wife) stitched him back together. But it is said that she cries every year when she remembers what Set did to Osiris, and her tears make the Nile flood.

The Pyramids of Giza

Tell ya'll the story of Amenhotep...
Amenhotep IV was a powerful player. He made a big name for himself and caused lots of controversy in Egypt by declaring that there was only one god, Aton. He declared all the other gods false. In doing this, he robbed the powerful class of priests of much of their authority.

I'm one of lots of gods: polytheism...
The ancient Egyptians, like most other antique cultures, believed in a host of gods and goddesses. They were very religious, and used gods to explain many natural phenomena, from the creation of the Earth to the movement of the sun. People everywhere thought that they had to win the favor of the gods to have a prosperous life. And there were many to please. A half dozen of them represented the sun alone – rising, setting, traveling. The Egyptians had gods of crocodiles, cows, cats, frogs. They had gods of measurement, gods who watched over the inner organs of the dead, and gods of mummification. The most important gods were Ra, god of the sun, who was considered the creator; Osiris, lord of the afterlife; Isis, goddess of magic; Amon, Theban King of all gods. Imagine trying to say your prayers at night!

And that one god was the sun god...
Amenhotep declared himself the sole voice of the sun-disc god Aton, and he changed his own name to show it. **Akhenaton** means "spirit of Aton." Though he imposed the worship of a sole god on the people, there was a big boom in the arts during his rule.

The priests and all of their gods, they came back...
After he died future pharaohs went back to polytheism, which made all the priests happy – they got their old jobs back.

HISTORY SPEAKS

"Egypt has more wonders in it than any other country in the world and provides more works that defy description than any other place."

- Herodotus

CHAPTER 5:
IT GOES ROUND AND ROUND

Ancient India: 2500 BC to 400 BC

The God Shiva in Fierce Form

INTRO

You do not know how far away your enemy is. You only know that if he sees you, he will kill you. But there are other dangers in this jungle, where the trees and bushes and leaves are so thick you can hardly see someone 10 feet away. There are tigers who, they say, love the taste of human flesh. There are snakes, too, with poisons your doctors and priests can't save you from. But your enemy has done something even more dangerous; his army has trained elephants for war. So when the soldiers come, they don't come on foot. They come on the backs of mighty war elephants and ride right over you. Welcome to India!

IT GOES ROUND AND ROUND

LYRICS

It goes round and round, goes round and round, till it what?

In the land before time,
Before there were dates,
India started with tectonic plates.
It bumped into China,
Made the Himalayas,
So tall, they protect us
From invaders.
Two rivers flow,
Indus and the Ganges,
Indus is in the west;
Ganges streams east.
In the Indus valley,
There were twin cities,
Mohenjo-daro and Harappa.
They built these cities
On a grid like New York,
And they had extra grain
For when the food's short.
The wind and rain came
With monsoons,
But they didn't stink, kid,
They built bathrooms!

It goes round and round,
It goes round and round,
Till it all comes back again.

Aryans came through the
Mountains to a new spot,
From the west,
And they "Hit 'Em Up" like Tupac.
Their chariots surge,
They're invaders,
They have a literature,

CONTEXT AND BACKGROUND

It bumped into China, made the Himalayas...

The world hasn't always looked the way it looks now. Land doesn't stay still but slowly shifts around on **tectonic plates**. India's plate was once part of Africa, but over millions of years, it slid off of Africa, across the sea, and slammed up against Asia. In doing this, it created a huge mountain range, the biggest in the world. These are the **Himalayas**, which is where you find Mount Everest.

Those massive peaks make a nice wall, cutting India off from the rest of the world. India is a peninsula, jutting down between the Arabian Sea and the Indian Ocean. It's surrounded by water on three sides and topped off by the biggest mountains on the planet on the fourth.

Two rivers flow, Indus and the Ganges...

Rushing down from the mountains are the **Indus and Ganges rivers**, which bring massive volumes of water to the countryside, making for great farming opportunities. This moisture, combined with the fact that India gets more rain than just about anywhere in the world, gives the area a moist, humid climate and lots of thick jungles.

In the Indus valley, there were twin cities...

The first people to migrate to the **Indus River Valley** were hunters who came from Africa, probably around 40,000 BC. For tens of thousands of years they followed animals around, until about 2500 BC, when they finally figured out

37

that the fertile soil around them would make ideal farmland.

The farmers here discovered the same things that farmers elsewhere had — irrigation makes for abundant crops; surpluses lead to trade and commerce; houses and villages make living easier. They built villages and by about 2300 BC, a large city had been built. Named for the present-day city of Harappa in Pakistan, the ancient **civilization of Harappa** was one of the most developed in the world in its day, a very happening place. It included the city of Harappa and another big urban area — **Mohenjo-daro**, about 300 miles away on another section of river. Even though they were far apart, the two cities had striking similarities.

They built these cities on a grid like New York...

Mohenjo-daro and Harappa were quite advanced for their day. Both were actually laid out with grids of streets that made right angles. Streets were paved and were home to stone houses, some of which were three or four stories high. Big fortresses stood near each city to provide protection.

And they had extra grain for when the food's short...

The people had weights, measures and a currency so they could trade. The government may have stored food in case of shortages. They were perhaps the first people to make garments out of cotton.

The Harappans used **pictographs**, drawings and symbols that represented ideas, to write. There were about 370 separate glyphs, or symbols, used. Close to 2,500 seals have been recovered from cities across India and Pakistan.

FLOCAB SPITS FACTS LIKE AN ALMANAC

Civilizations and groups come and go, but some, like the Harappans, disappear in more mysterious ways than others. History is filled with such strange disappearances. Here are a few:

Maya: Once powerful, this early American empire had disappeared by the time the Spanish sailed over. Mayans had reverted to living in small, separate villages. Possible culprit: internal fighting.

Minoa: These people built amazing cities on the island of Crete, just below Greece. They even rebuilt after a volcano destroyed many of their towns, but 50 years later, they abandoned them altogether. Possible culprit: Who knows?

Atlantis: Ever heard of the lost city of Atlantis? It's a famous city that no archaeologist has ever found. There's a simple reason for this: It never existed. It was just something that Plato dreamed up and wrote about. Possible culprit: It's fictional.

LYRICS continued

And it's called the Vedas.
It's about gods, it's written Sanskrit,
But we've translated so we
Understand it.
But back then some wise men
Called Brahman,
Were like priests,
Wanted to be uncommon.
When you take away religion
From the people,
Then the priests get powerful,
It's not equal.
So the Brahman rose up like
Pinnocchio's nose
Goes up when he says things that
Are not true.
Plus, the Aryans were more light-
Skinned than the Indians
Who lived there before those guys
Came through.
So what caste are you?
What class are you?
Are you the Brahman,
The priests controlling the things?
The soldiers and their wives,
Kshatriya?
Or merchants and farm owners,
Vaishya?
Sudra working on farms,
Staying out of trouble?
Or below it all, Dalit,
The "untouchables"?

Hook

Vedas were written by the priests,
That started Hinduism,
And here's what it means:
Brahman, a universal spirit,
Is everywhere at all times,
Can you feel it?

The wind and rain came with monsoons...
For complex reasons, a big wind, called a **monsoon,** blows north through India every summer for a few months. It brings lots of rain and thunderstorms with it, so summers are the rainy seasons. These monsoons bring lots of water to Indian crops, which helps the economy.

But they didn't stink, kid, they built bathrooms...
Both cities had another great invention: sewer systems to carry all human waste out of the city. Almost no other cities had a sewer system at this time. I'm sure you can imagine that those other cities smelled really, really bad. Harappan civilization disappeared sometime after 2000 BC for reasons unknown.

Aryans came through the mountains to a new spot...
Don't confuse the Aryans of ancient India with the Aryans of Adolf Hitler's master race. (It was Hitler who was confused.) These **Aryans** were Indo-Europeans who migrated from Central Asia through Iran to the Indus River Valley around 1500 BC. They were a nomadic and warlike people.

Their chariots surge, they're invaders...
The Aryans rode in on chariots and horses, which are native to the steppes of Central Asia. By about 800 BC they'd made their way to the Ganges River, using weapons of iron to conquer more and more territory. Many of the Aryans settled around the Ganges. They brought their culture and their language, known as **Sanskrit,** as well as their gods and early

Hinduism. They also brought their social hierarchy, known as the caste system.

They have a literature, and it's called the Vedas...

The **Vedas** were ancient Indian texts that became the basis for the Hindu religion. There were four major ones: the Rig Veda, Sama Veda, Yajur Veda, and Atharva Veda. The Rig Veda is often considered the oldest piece of literature that still exists, dating back to at least 3700 BC, although some historians think it's much older than that. It has the earliest mentions of astronomy, astrology and many other metaphysical "sciences." AS a group, the Vedas explored the relationship of the human soul to the material world. In them can be found the earliest mentions of yoga, meditation and mantras.

Then the priests get powerful, it's not equal...

In cultures that believe in god or gods (as nearly all do), there are nearly always people who claim that they alone can speak with their god or interpret the messages of the gods. These people become priests. As the doorway to the gods, they usually become very powerful and often very rich. This is exactly the situation for the **Brahman** in India. They interpreted the Vedas and guided the customs of Hinduism. And they became big shots.

Plus, the Aryans were more light-skinned, than the Indians...

At first, as in other cultures, there were two classes of people in India: nobles and commoners. Indo-Aryans later added a third category, the "darks," probably reserved for the darker-skinned people they conquered. But the caste system wasn't really about race. It was about dividing people into classes and making sure everyone stayed where they began. Who do you think set up that system - the people at the top or at the bottom?

So what caste are you? What class are you...

All men and women were definitely not created equal, according to ancient Indian rules. Their society was soon divided into four classes or **castes**. It was very hierarchical -there was a very definite high class and very definite lower classes and no movement from one to another.

Are you the Brahman, the priests controlling the things...

At the very top were the Brahman, who were the leaders and the priests. Only the men in this caste could attend school.

The soldiers and their wives, Kshatriya...

On the next rung were the Kshatriya, the soldiers. (Women couldn't fight but the wives of soldiers still belonged to this class.)

Or merchants and farm owners, Vaishya...

Beneath the warriors were the businessmen, tradespeople, and farmers — the Vaishya. This caste was able to own land.

Sudra working on farms, staying out of trouble...

The next class, Sudra, included the servants, clerks, and farmhands. There were huge numbers of these folks.

LYRICS continued

You've got to have good karma,
Do good work,
So when you're reborn,
You won't be born a bird.
Reincarnation:
You always come back,
As something different,
So you better know that.

You rhyme soft, kid, I spit harder,
More enlightened than Siddhartha,
A Hindu prince bothered by the
Suffering on the streets,
So he gave away his stuff,
With nothing to eat.
Practiced yoga and meditated
To be free,
Sat beneath a fig tree
And he found peace.
In a flash like the "bloop"
On your computer,
This kid Siddhartha
Became Buddha.
Found Nirvana in his mind;
That's a perfect place,
Where suffering is erased
Without a trace.
So no matter if you sit
Behind bars in prison,
Heaven is in your mind;
That's Buddhism.

Hook

And Buddha says:
"All that we are is the result of
What we have thought. The mind
Is everything. What we think, we
Become."

Or below it all, Dalit, the untouchables...
Beneath the Sudra was the group known as the Dalit, or "the untouchables." They were the freemen and women who held the worst jobs in society. They existed below the caste system, and people were not supposed to have any contact with them.

Vedas were written by the priests, that started Hinduism...
Hinduism is the world's oldest major religion that is still practiced. A group of diverse beliefs and traditions, Hinduism has no single founder. It is the world's third largest religion, following Christianity and Islam, with approximately one billion adherents, most of whom live in India and Nepal.

Brahman, a universal spirit, is everywhere at all times...
Brahman (spelled the same as the word for *priests*, but with a different meaning) is the unchanging, infinite reality that exists in all matter, energy, time, space, being and everything beyond in this universe. To achieve enlightenment, most Hindus believe that you must realize that you are and always will be made of pure energy - pure Brahman.

You've got to have good karma, do good work...
Your **karma** is the energy you create when you do something that is either right or wrong. Doing something wrong, like lying, creates bad karma, while doing something good, like helping someone, creates good karma.

FLOCAB SPITS FACTS LIKE AN ALMANAC

Buddhism isn't just a popular religion in India, China and Japan. It's practiced all over the world, and seems to hold a special attraction for Hollywood celebrities. Actors Orlando Bloom (*The Lord of the Rings*), Naomi Watts (*King Kong*), Uma Thurman (*Kill Bill*) and Keanu Reeves (*The Matrix*) are all Buddhists. Jennifer Lopez told reporters she's given Buddhism serious thought, and the Beastie Boys' MCA has even written songs about the religion.

In the song "Bodhisattva Vow," he raps, "With the interconnectedness that we share as one / Every action that we take affects everyone."

Reincarnation: You always come back…

Karma is important because it determines what you will come back as in your next life. Hindus believe in **reincarnation**, the idea that a person's soul is reborn again and again into different bodies, including animals. Basically, you go round and round, trying to live a better life, until you get it right. You might come back in your next life as a squirrel or a king, but you have to live life right in order to reach enlightenment and Nirvana.

A Hindu prince bothered by the suffering on the streets…

Siddhartha was a young, rich Indian prince born in about 560 BC. He wasn't happy with his life as a Hindu; he sought more answers than he felt that religion could offer. One day he left his family and his riches behind, and decided that the secret of life was not to be reincarnated over and over but to find enlightenment, the state of being free from suffering.

This kid Siddhartha became Buddha…

Siddhartha wandered around India looking for life's answers, but not finding any. He stopped and sat under a big, beautiful tree on the Ganges River and meditated. For seven weeks he sat under that tree, until he became enlightened. After that he was known as the Buddha, or "enlightened one." He spent the rest of his life sharing his ideas with people, founding a whole new religion: **Buddhism.**

Found Nirvana in his mind, that's a perfect place…

Nirvana is the highest goal of a

IT GOES ROUND AND ROUND

LYRICS continued

"Thousands of candles can be Lit from a single candle, and The life of the candle will not Be shortened. Happiness never decreases by Being shared."

Buddhist. Some people simply call it enlightenment. Nirvana happens when a Buddhist is finally free of suffering and all worldly problems - he or she has broken the cycle of reincarnation and is in a state of peace.

After the Lyrics

In 326 BC, Alexander the Great invaded India, and spread his huge empire all the way to the Indus River Valley. But when he returned to Babylon in 324 BC, an Indian ruler named **Chandragupta** overthrew a bunch of his generals in the Punjab area and set up the largest Indian kingdom yet, called the **Mauryan Empire**.

Ashoka was another famous ruler of the Mauryan Empire. He expanded the kingdom of India — but at a terrible cost. They say his battlefield victories were so brutal and bloody that he eventually renounced war altogether. He became a Buddhist and was instrumental in spreading the faith to millions of others across Central Asia.

CHAPTER 6:

CHINESE KNOWLEDGE

Ancient China: 750 BC to 220 AD

INTRO

The Chinese creation myth is based on a character named Pan Gu. He lived inside an egg for 18,000 years, then decided to break out. When he did, the light, clear part of the egg floated up and became the sky, and the rest oozed out and became the ground. When he stood up, Pan Gu found that his head hit the sky while his feet stayed on the earth. The earth and sky began to grow 10 feet a day and Pan Gu did as well. This went on for another 18,000 years until Pan Gu was millions of feet tall. When he died, his eyes became the sun and moon, his last breath the wind, his blood the oceans and his body the mountains.

The Terracotta Warriors

CHINESE KNOWLEDGE

LYRICS

On the other side of the globe,
The mountains rise,
The sea waves,
And the deserts stay dry.
Rivers crisscross this
Chinese landscape,
Didn't have pizza,
Had green onion pancakes.
Shang Dynasty, it came first,
Made jade dragon bowls,
That's some handiwork.
Chinese priest dropped knowledge
To excite the crowd,
Someone's like, "He's smart, we
Should write this down."
But how? Various Chinese say
"Tree" differently,
But we all draw the same
Character for tree.
So you can say "Peking,"
And I'll say "Beijing,"
But it's one city,
So it means the same thing.
Chinese believed an all-powerful
Dragon lived in the seas,
And could fly.
And so the dynasties took this
Symbol; they're like, "It's simple,
I'll make it mine."

Kick the knowledge,
Kick the Chinese knowledge.

Zhou, Qin, and Han dynasties
Rolled in,
Claim a mandate from heaven,
Like they're chosen.
That's a typical tactic rulers use,

CONTEXT AND BACKGROUND

The sea waves, and the deserts stay dry...
China is so large that it has all kinds of environments. You can roast in the desert, swim in the salty sea, or climb some of the tallest mountains on Earth. In fact, the region's geography kept the ancient Chinese pretty much where they were. They were very isolated and didn't know much about the other cultures growing in other parts of the world. Most people in ancient times settled along the **Huang He River** (also known as the **Yellow River**). This curving waterway, at 3,000 miles in length, is one of the longest in the world. For years, the Chinese would build their homes next to the river, only to have them wiped away when it flooded. This went on for a long time before they too discovered the concept of irrigation, and early civilization was born.

Rivers crisscross this Chinese landscape...
You the great. No, Yu the great. The founder of the **Xia Dynasty**, Yu is still a legend in China for "conquering the flood." In other words, he harnessed the mighty power of the Yellow River, transforming it from a destroyer into the very foundation of civilization.

Shang Dynasty, it came first...
The **Shang Dynasty** is the first Chinese dynasty that historians really know much about. The Shang culture dates back to around 1750 BC. The Chinese were then making the transition from being a Neolithic people — early farmers — to a civilized one. The Shang

45

FLOCAB SPITS FACTS LIKE AN ALMANAC

Boom, baby.

The Chinese first began using gunpowder in 200 AD, long before anyone else had even begun to think about exploding powders. They first used it in fireworks to celebrate special events. By 800 AD they'd realized the awesome power of the substance and had begun using it in warfare as bombs and rockets.

How's it shaking?

The ancient Chinese were a very inventive people. They came up with an early compass, made paper, discovered gunpowder, and put together the world's first seismograph as certain parts of China were very prone to earthquakes. So during the Han Dynasty (c. 206 BC–220 AD), a creative tinkerer made a tremor gauge. This was a bronze statue with nine dragons laid out in a circle. In the mouth of each one was a small ball. An earthquake of a certain magnitude would cause a ball to fall. The people could tell roughly which direction the temblor hit by which way the ball fell.

were starting to write, they worked with bronze tools, and they lived in cities.

But we all draw the same character for tree...

The ancient Chinese did their writing by drawing and carving, like so many other ancient cultures. Only instead of using rock tablets, they used bones, called **oracle bones** because they were thought to tell people's fortunes, long before the fortune cookie came into play. Communication was also done using shells. Archaeologists have discovered more than 10,000 oracle bones and have used them to learn a lot about what the early Chinese were thinking about.

So you can say Peking, and I'll say Beijing...

Maybe you've heard of two Chinese cities: Peking and Beijing. But you can save yourself some money and visit both at the same time, because Peking *is* Beijing (and vice versa). There are two names in English because there are different ways of pronouncing the word in Chinese. But this is why **Chinese characters** are so important. The Chinese alphabet doesn't use letters to write out the sounds of different words; it uses characters that represent the words. This makes it easier for them to communicate with people who pronounce words differently, but it makes learning to read and write difficult because every student must memorize thousands of characters.

Claim a mandate from heaven, like they're chosen...

The Egyptian pharaohs told their subjects they were gods on earth. The ancient Chinese kings had similar

LYRICS continued

They claim that God wants them
To rule the roost, but it's a ruse.
Anyway, the Zhou were cool,
Developed iron,
They've got the strongest tools.
The Qins didn't have big chins
Like Jay Leno,
They built a big wall,
Block by block like Legos.
The Wall of China
Later became great
To stop the nomadic tribes,
Who liked to invade.
But the Qin were mean,
Didn't want to be criticized,
If you did, they would
Bury you alive.
The Han Dynasty
Had that civil service,
Want to work for the man,
You pass an exam.
Big Chinese peace
Means the Chinese streets,
Were safe to trade the things
The Chinese need.
The Silk Road that
They built though,
Connects Asia with Greece and
Rome to trade their silk clothes.
But what did they believe?
They had yin and the yang,
Two forces to form a balance
Like a woman and man.
Confucius, don't get confused, kid,
He said, respect your parents,
They're not useless.
Now Taoism is the "way of nature,"
Don't pray, meditate, and you'll
Get the flavor.

Hook

ideas, but believed they were given the right to rule by heaven. They called this the **Mandate of Heaven**. If a king was bad, his right to rule was withdrawn from heaven and given to another leader. This is also how the Chinese helped explain their dynasties, which sometimes moved from one to the next.

Zhou were cool, developed iron...

From Northwest China, the **Zhou** tribe rolled in and overthrew the Shang. The Zhou quickly set up their own dynasty, claiming that the Shang had lost their Mandate of Heaven by being cruel and corrupt. The Zhou expanded internal trade and printed copper coins. They also introduced iron, a strong metal that helped farmers work better and faster. Eventually the Zhou lost control of China, and various states fighting for power.

The Qins didn't have big chins like Jay Leno...

You didn't want to mess with the **Qin**, who came from a small state in the western part of China. During the **Warring States period**, from about 475 to 221 BC, no single power was in command of China. All of the states jockeyed for control, often in bloody ways. Out of this scramble rose the Qin.

They unified a huge chunk of China for the first time and ruled for just 15 years. But they had a great impact on Chinese society. Qin, also written Ch'in, is probably the origin of the word *China*.

Historians found a number of things interesting about the Qin. They were great warriors and among the first to use cavalry (warriors on horses).

They standardized many things, from money to the language and writing. They started building the Great Wall of China. And they had absolute power over their subjects. They were the people who came up with the strict philosophy known as Legalism.

They built a wall, block by block like Legos...

Ancient China's most famous feature can still be seen from outer space: **The Great Wall**. This mammoth structure was built to keep out the Mongol invaders from the north. The wall averages about 25 feet tall and is more than 3,000 miles long, so it did a pretty good job of keeping out unwanted neighbors. The Qin didn't build the entire wall themselves; they joined a lot of smaller, shorter walls that already existed in parts of the kingdom into one giant barrier. Some parts were brick; others were grass and mud. Each dynasty made changes to the wall. During the Ming period, more than 1 million soldiers manned the Great Wall at one time. In recent years, scientists have dug up more than 600 miles of wall that had been previously buried.

FLOCAB SPITS FACTS LIKE AN ALMANAC

Whereas Christianity has the Ten Commandments, Buddhism had its **Eightfold Plan**. This guide to righteous living went something like this:

People should try:
1. To know the truth.
2. To resist evil.
3. To not say anything to hurt others.
4. To respect life, property, and morality.
5. To work at a job that does not injure others.
6. To try to free one's mind from evil.
7. To be in control of one's feelings and thoughts.
8. To practice appropriate forms of concentration.

If you're able to adhere to these principles, you're on the **Middle Way**. Buddhists believed the Middle Way — not the hard or the way, but somewhere in between — was the proper path to take in life.

But the Qin were mean, didn't want to be criticized...

Legalism was not a very pleasant philosophy, but it was a brutally efficient one. It was based on the idea that rulers are wise and people are stupid. Strict laws had to be in place to govern the masses; otherwise there would be chaos. The Qin got rid of all of the leaders who governed the Warring States they had conquered and installed their own governors. And with them, they set up rules, rules, rules, and more rules. You want to question authority? That would get you in deep trouble. The Qin broke society down into groups of families, usually 5 to 10 depending on their sizes. Each group had the responsibility of keeping everyone in their group in line. If not, they all suffered very harsh penalties. One group of 400 scholars, for example, was buried alive.

The Han dynasty had that civil service...

Many of the biggest advances in Chinese culture came during the **Han Dynasty** (206 BC-220 AD). After the repressive Qin era, the Han were a breath of fresh air. Instead of imposing its will upon the people, the government actually softened a little and became something of a meritocracy. If you wanted to work for the government, you had to pass an exam - it wasn't enough just to say your uncle already worked for the government.

You've probably heard of **acupuncture**, in which a doctor pokes you with needles to help cure you of certain ailments. This is when it got its start. Buddhism was introduced from India at about this time as well.

The Silk Road that they built though, connects Asia with Greece and Rome...

No, it wasn't a street lined with fabric. It wasn't any single road at all, really. **The Silk Road** was the name given to the trade routes across China. The Chinese discovered during the Han Dynasty that the Romans liked their silks and spices. They wanted the Romans' gold, so traders began to traverse the 4,000 miles between the two regions. Most of these merchants only went part of the way, but the goods made it back and forth, despite the fact that the travel took people across some of the world's toughest landscapes: the tallest mountains, the coldest deserts. The Silk Road spread knowledge as well, and opened up whole new worlds to the Chinese.

They had yin and the yang...

The idea of **yin and yang** comes from an ancient Chinese belief that the world is made up of a series of opposite forces that, taken together, form a balance. Yin is female and dark; yang is male and bright. They do not oppose each other like good and evil, but actually need each other to create harmony.

Confucius, don't get confused, kid, he said respect your parents...

Your mom and dad probably wished you studied the philosopher Confucius a little more. **Confucius** created some very powerful philosophies based around the importance of family. In ancient China, you honored your parents above anyone else, and you did your best to bring respect to your family name.

They're not useless...
In ancient China you always had to listen to your mom and dad — even when they were dead. Family was so important that people believed the spirits of their relatives were able to pass judgment from beyond the grave. They could offer assistance to their living family members and bring down their wrath on those they believed were dishonoring the family name. So it wasn't just your mom telling you to clean your room — it was her dead great-grandfather Li, too.

Taoism is the "way of nature"...
Go with the flow: That's the basic idea of **Taoism**. It was a very popular philosophy in ancient China. Some people consider it a religion, but it's more a way of thinking than anything else. The basic premise of Taoism is that people should live in harmony with the universe as much as possible. One of its most common metaphors is that people should be like a river that flows around obstacles rather than tries to fight its way through them. Tao means "The Way," and is thought to be an invisible guiding force that exists all around us in nature. The philosophy's founder was Lao Tzu, a thinker who lived in 600 BC. People still follow his principles today, even Winnie the Pooh.

HISTORY SPEAKS

"Everything has its beauty but not everyone sees it."
— Confucius

"Don't open a shop unless you like to smile."
— Chinese Proverb

CHAPTER 7:

ART OF WAR
& LEGALISM
INTERLUDE
600 BC & 250 BC

LYRICS

"All warfare is based on deception. So, when able to attack, we must seem unable; when using our forces, we must seem inactive; when we are near, we must make the enemy believe we are far away; when far away, we must make him believe we are near. Hold out baits to entice the enemy. Feign disorder, and crush him.

To fight and conquer in all your battles is not supreme excellence; supreme excellence consists in breaking the enemy's resistance without fighting."

That's Sun-Tzu, *The Art of War*.

CONTEXT AND BACKGROUND

Sun-Tzu wrote his legendary military treatise ***The Art of War*** in the 6th century BC. The book's 13 chapters tackle various aspects of warfare and military strategy, making it one of the oldest books on military tactics in the world. The book has been required reading for the Chinese army since the Song Dynasty. With its more recent popularity, *The Art of War* has been extremely influential in military thinking and business strategy, as well as among rappers and professional video game players.

Sun-Tzu himself was a landless Chinese aristocrat who lived at the time of Confucius. Instead of devoting his life to academics like many other aristocrats, Sun-Tzu worked as a military consultant, a kind of general-for-hire. According to some accounts, he once trained a battalion of all-female troops, who eventually became talented soldiers under him. After a series of victories on the battlefield, Sun-Tzu disappeared into the mountains somewhere. As is clear from his book, he always preferred peace.

ART OF WAR & LEGALISM

"When a sage governs a state, he does not rely on the people to do good out of their own will. Instead, He sees to it that they are not allowed to do what is not good. If he relies on people to do good out of their own will, within the borders of the state not even 10 persons can be counted on [to do good]. Yet, if one sees to it that they are not allowed to do what is not good, the whole state can be brought to uniform order...The wisdom of the people is useless: They have the minds of little infants!"

That's Han Fei-tzu.

Han Fei-tzu (also Han Fei, 280-233 BC) was a philosopher who developed the philosophy behind **Legalism**, the hard-line, totalitarian policy practiced by the Qin dynasty. There are three important ideas in Legalism, all of which are designed to have one single ruler controlling all the people. The first idea is law: Laws must punish those who do wrong, and reward those who do right. The second idea is tactics: The ruler must employ tactics and secrets to make sure the people do not understand his motives, which will allow him to stay in power longer. The third is legitimacy: A ruler must understand that the title of "ruler" is more important than the ruler himself.

Under Legalism, the Qin rulers cracked down on those who opposed them, and tried to keep their movements secret from the public. Some would say that similar things exist in China today: The government puts serious limits on free speech.

After many years in the Qin court, Han Fei-tzu was persecuted by his colleagues and forced to drink poison in prison.

A Bamboo Edition of *The Art of War*

CHAPTER 8:

LIKE A PERSIAN

The Persian Empire: 550 BC to 331 BC

INTRO

First understand that Persia is **Iran** and vice versa. The land now known as Iran was called Persia by most people until 1935 when its King said, "Please call us Iran." So most people do.

In 2001, American President George W. Bush said that Iran was part of an "axis of evil." Iran's president, in turn, said that "we will soon experience a world without the United States." In the years before and since, there has been lots of tension between America in the West and Iran in the East. Today's tension and clash of cultures echo the past, namely, a series of incredible wars between the Greeks and the Persians.

It's important to avoid thinking of any group in such simple terms as "us" versus "them." In fact, we learn this lesson by studying the history of Persia itself. Just ask Cyrus the Great.

Persian Emperor Darius III

LYRICS

Let's take it back to the sixth
Century BC,
When the Persians mastered
The Middle East.
Before wars were fought digitally,
They said, "Send in the cavalry,"
Rhat's literally.
In the desert land, where you could
Get sand in your sandwich,
An empire was born
And spread by the sword.
The Persians were the ancestors of
Modern Iranians,
And they had the greatest army,
Always training them
To take on neighboring states of
Mesopotamia,
They reached the Himalayas and
Conquered the rest of Arabia.
Persian secret weapon was the
Special forces, "The Immortals,"
Warriors who would ride into war
On impressive horses and leave a
Mess of corpses, in their wake,
Led by Cyrus the Great.
He freed Hebrews from Babylon,
"Thanks, Cyrus."
Not Hannah Montana;
Cyrus was the nicest.

Like a Persian:
Tough since the very first times,
Smart since the very first rhymes.
We're the army comin'
And you can hardly summon
The strength to stand up,
We're Persian.

CONTEXT AND BACKGROUND

Let's take it back to the sixth century BC...
Various groups had populated the land we now call Iran by 600 BC. The west of the country was a beautiful, mountainous land with green valleys and rugged peaks, which gave way to desert sands in the east. The different groups who lived there were brought together under the leadership of one charismatic and charming guy: Cyrus the Great.

When the Persians mastered the Middle East...
When **Cyrus the Great** (585-529 BC) took power in Persia, the kingdom, near Mesopotamia, was relatively small. Within 20 years, Cyrus had expanded it to include a vast territory, all the way from the Himalayas to what is now Turkey and down past Israel to the Arabian Peninsula. It was an astonishing accomplishment.

And they had the greatest army, always training them...
Cyrus had set up the largest empire the world had ever seen. He built an incredibly strong and effective army. Persian power, like that of nearly every empire, was spread by the sword. His successors would build an even larger army and expand the empire further still, taking Egypt and parts of India and Greece.

The special forces, "The Immortals"...
The Persian army was led by a group of 10,000 soldiers called **The Immortals**. They must have seemed immortal because everywhere they went,

they were unstoppable. Part of their success was due to the incredible loyalty they had for Cyrus, but they also had a fast cavalry, able to strike with speed. The cavalry, or mounted warriors, attacked not only with horses but with bows and arrows as well – the same technique that the armies of Attila the Hun and Genghis Khan would later use so devastatingly.

Led by Cyrus the Great...

Cyrus the Great was one of the world's finest military men - one would have to be to conquer the Babylonians, Assyrians, Jews, Syrians, Phoenicians, Lydians, Turks Greeks, and everyone else he managed to overthrow. He was also supposedly a just and fair ruler. He allowed each of the cultures that he incorporated into his empire to continue living the way they had been living; they could practice their religions and continue their traditions.

He freed Hebrews from Babylon...

Cyrus was respected by many of the groups that he conquered and united, but he was especially important to the Jews. He issued a kind of emancipation proclamation freeing the Jews from slavery, and told them to rebuild their temple in Jerusalem. For this reason, the Jewish Bible refers to Cyrus as a "messiah," a leader chosen by God. He is the only non-Jew to get this distinction.

Not Hannah Montana; Cyrus was the nicest...

Cyrus also created an artifact known as the **Cyrus cylinder**, a cylinder-shaped stone covered in writing. It was written in cuneiform, and it recounted some of Cyrus's hopes, as well as his belief that people should be free to

FLOCAB SPITS FACTS LIKE AN ALMANAC

The Madness of Cambyses

According to the important Greek historian Herodotus, Cambyses went crazy. While in Egypt, he became paranoid and jealous when the Egyptians started celebrating a sacred bull that had appeared in their town. Fuming mad at this "bull-god," Cambyses had the bull brought to him and stabbed it with his sword. Then Cambyses ordered that anyone caught worshipping the bull should be put to death. This did not make him very popular in Egypt.

worship their own gods and practice their own traditions. Some historians have traced America's Bill of Rights back to the Cyrus cylinder.

Like a Persian...

The founder of Zoroastrianism, **Zarathustra** was most likely from a province in what is now Afghanistan. Very little is known about his life, though most historians agree that he was a prophet who had visions, and one of the first to propose that there was only a single god in the centuries before Jesus. His philosophy was strongly based on good vs. evil, and was the most popular religion during the Persian Empire. Some religious scholars have noted similarities between Zoroastrianism and Hindu texts. Some people in India and Iran

LYRICS continued

Cambyses inherited the kingdom
In 529 BC,
And he was quite pleased.
He wanted to extend the
Empire's reach,
But he spent a little too much
Time overseas.
Conquered Egypt,
But his leadership was not,
As strategic as his father's.
He left his brother running things for
Too long and lost his allegiance,
Maybe his brother was a fake,
But either way.
The new king of Persia was
Darius the Great,
He knew how to collect coins
And build up trade.
But try as he might,
Darius couldn't increase
The empire's size by
Invading Greece.
Greco-Persian Wars began in 490,
Three hundred Spartans stopped
Them at Thermopylae.
A Greek traitor's hand showed 'em
The place to land,
But this was the home of the
Marathon Man.
And Greeks fought with hoplites.
"That's not right!"
And a storm at sea destroyed a
Third of the fleet.
Even Xerxes I couldn't
Conquer Greece,
'Cause they were too strong,
And had bomb philosophies.

Hook

continue to practice the faith.

**Cambyses inherited the kingdom in
529 BC...**
After Cyrus died, his son **Cambyses**
took the throne. His dad had
conquered the Middle East, and so
Cambyses thought he should try to
conquer Egypt, the only remaining
independent state in that part of the
world. So Cambyses headed off to
Egypt, leaving his brother Smerdis
in charge of running the eastern
provinces.

**He left his brother running things for too
long...**
Cambyses conquered Egypt with his
mighty army. Some accounts say that
having killed the pharaoh, Cambyses
started to dress in the pharaoh's
clothes.
    But here is where the
drama really began. Back in
Persia, Cambyses's brother Smerdis
was grabbing power in Asia and
proclaiming himself the Persian
emperor. Some people claimed that
the man doing this wasn't even the
real Smerdis at all, but an imposter;
they said the real Smerdis was already
dead. Either way, Cambyses was
scared to march against this "Smerdis"
guy, and he was slowly losing his mind.
During this time, Cambyses either died
by accident or he killed himself.

**The new king of Persia was Darius the
Great...**
Darius stepped up and led the army
against Smerdis, killing him and then
claiming the throne. **Darius** was only
loosely related to Cambyses and
Cyrus, but in 521 he became emperor
anyway. He became known as **"the
shopkeeper,"** and introduced coined

money and a good postal service. He divided the empire into easy-to-manage states and moved the capital to the city of Persepolis.

The empire's size by invading Greece...

But Darius wasn't happy just keeping his empire running smoothly. In 490 BC, he attacked Greece. Their empire bordered his on his western flank, and he wanted it. Plus, he was unhappy with the Greeks for siding with the Ionians, who had rebelled against his control. He was able to take several Greek cities, but the Athenians put up a great fight. This was called the First Persian War, or **First Greco-Persian War**.

But this was the home of the Marathon Man...

In the First Persian War, the Persian invasion force landed at Marathon. Though fighting a much larger army, the Greeks eventually won. The idea of a **marathon** (a 26.2-mile run) comes

The Greeks

from this time, as a Greek messenger ran the 26 miles to Athens to tell the city of the victory — before he collapsed and died. It was the first marathon.

And Greeks fought with hoplites (that's not right)...

Most soldiers standing on their feet were no match for a warrior on a horse. To change that, the Greeks developed the **hoplites**, a type of Greek foot soldier. These soldiers had large shields and long spears and would group themselves very closely together in what is known as a **phalanx** formation. When cavalry came charging in, the hoplites would raise their weapons at an angle, creating a virtual wall of spears. They were very effective.

And a storm at sea destroyed a third of the fleet...

The Second Persian War began 10 years later when Darius's son **Xerxes** wanted revenge on the Greeks. He attacked by land and sea against a coalition of Greek cities, including the Athenians, Spartans, and Corinthians. Xerxes was an interesting guy who built up the Persian army even more. Herodotus, a famous Greek historian, wrote that Xerxes's army, some two million men, would drink entire rivers dry. Herodotus also reported that when a bridge between Turkey and Greece broke, Xerxes beheaded the engineer and ordered that the river be lashed 300 times as punishment.

Even Xerxes the First couldn't conquer Greece...

Amazingly, a scrappy group of Greek warriors was able to fight off the giant army that had conquered all of the

Middle East. Most famously, a group of 300 Spartans held off thousands of Persian soldiers at Thermopylae, a narrow passage between cliffs. When one Spartan heard that the Persians were so numerous that their arrows would "blot out the sun," he replied, "Then we will fight in the shade." Even today, "in the shade" is the motto of a division in the Greek army, and the story has been the basis of books, comics and movies.

HISTORY SPEAKS

"Cyrus the Great is genuinely one of history's towering figures. America's own founders, such as Thomas Jefferson, were influenced by Cyrus the Great in the field of human rights."
– Ted Koppel, ABC News

CHAPTER 9:

PARTY AT THE PARTHENON

Ancient Greece: 800 BC to 300 BC

INTRO

We are all Greek. You may not descend from the people who once lived on the sea-surrounded lands called Greece, but we owe a huge part of how we think and how we live in our country to the Greeks. Greeks created democracy, that amazing idea that the government should not be run by kings who happened to have "noble" blood, or dictators who happened to command the biggest army, but by the people. And the Greeks created logic, a careful way of thinking about arguments and words. Crazy as it sounds, it is logic that allows programmers to create video games. So the next time you play your Nintendo or Xbox, you can thank the Greeks.

PARTY AT THE PARTHENON

LYRICS

"Ladies and Gentlemen, accepting the lifetime achievement award on behalf of Greece, the one and only - Hercules."

"Ah, thank you very much. I deserve it. OK, everyone be quiet now, because I'm going to talk. I'm going to say thanks, I guess, to Greece, I guess, it's the cradle of civilization, OK. But we all know I made it famous.

"Ladies and Gentlemen..."

"Thank you, here I am. Appreciate that announcer. OK, a special shout to Mount Olympus, where I went to high school. OK, a lot of people there that didn't make it where I made it, so you know, you guys stink."

"Ladies and Gentlemen..."

"Oh, thanks, be quiet, please. Hello to my dad, Zeus. Uh, look at me now. Special shout to Pericles; thanks for the Golden Age, glad I could contribute. Shout out to Apollo, for the sun and my fabulous tan. Party at the Parthenon!"

Ancient Greece -
Cradle of civilization,
Divided into small kingdoms,

CONTEXT AND BACKGROUND

Ancient Greece - cradle of civilization...
On a map, Greece looks like a peninsula. And it is. But it's really more of a series of peninsulas, broken up by water. There are coves and inlets all over the place. The land dips into the Mediterranean and is flanked by the Ionian Sea to the west and the Aegean Sea to the east. In the seas are a constellation of islands, the biggest being Crete and Rhodes. Between all of this water is a hilly, rocky, and mountainous landscape. In ancient Greece, all of the bays and coves and peaks served to isolate each of the growing communities, which may be why they developed into independent kingdoms.

Divided into small kingdoms...
The ancient Greeks drew their inspiration from many different peoples, but two of the most prominent were the Minoans and the Mycenaeans. The **Mycenaeans** were an early civilization who lived on the large peninsula that forms the southern half of Greece. They were the first people to speak Greek, and they built forts all over the area. The **Mycenaean** civilization probably came after **Minoans,** who lived on the isle of Crete. They date back to 2000 BC and had a very advanced society for their time. They were famous for their seagoing expertise — they traded all over the eastern Mediterranean. Like the Harrapans, they disappeared for unclear reasons.

Or city-states with...

Imagine if you lived in a city that was also a country, with its own king, government, army, currency and everything else. That's how it was in early Greece with the many city-states that developed. By the Bronze Age, the area we now know as Greece was divided into many small kingdoms, each the size of a city and its surrounding countryside. The best known were Athens, Sparta, Corinth, Ithaca, Pylos, and Mycenae. The Greeks called these city-states **"polis,"** a word that's been incorporated into our language in *metropolis* and even *politics*.

City-states were originally formed for protection. Walled fortresses were built around cities, and people from nearby farms would race into the walls at any sign of trouble. Historians think of the city-state era in Greece as its classical age, the time when many of their greatest advancements and achievements were made.

A hill, with the city built on top of it...

City-states often had similar layouts. They were usually built on an **acropolis**, or hill, because hills were the most defensible positions. The walls were then built at the highest points. Inside, the city was typically organized around an **agora**, or marketplace, where the residents would come to trade, shop, or gather for socializing and meetings. Because they felt safe with the walls around them, they didn't

Hercules and Athena

Or city-states with
The best known being Athens,
Sparta, and Ithaca,
Corinth, Pylos, Mycenae.
Can you picture the Acropolis?
Walls to defend the populace,
A hill, with the city built on top of it.
To do some shopping,
You can hit the Agora,
But not in Sparta, 'cause they were
Trying to get their war up.
The only polis with
Permanent soldiers,
Helots were Mycenaean slaves
That they took over.
Let's keep it classical and take it
Back to Athens, where
They had the first government with
Citizens running it.
Democracy extended by Pericles,
The Greek leader that nobody
Could dare to be.
He built the Parthenon,
Ushered in the Golden Age,
And helped to define the Greece
That we all know today.

Yeah,
Bring your own Trireme tonight.
Dock it up at the
Party at the Parthenon!

Hey Achilles, how's your heel?
You're invited to the
Party at the Parthenon!

Think I might have a little mock-
Olympic games, you know, at the
Party at the Parthenon!

Just bring some hummus,

have to worry so much about defense anymore, which gave them the free time to work on art or found businesses. People often felt real attachment to their city-state and considered themselves Athenians, Spartans, or Corinthians rather than Greeks.

But not in Sparta, 'cause they were trying to get their war up...
Spartans were a military-obsessed people. Not much is known about them because they didn't write much. Presumably, they were too busy doing push-ups and wrestling. They lived in an area surrounded by mountains — a good wall of defense.

The only polis with permanent soldiers...
By most accounts, **Sparta** was the only city-state to have a permanent, full-time army. Most of the others had citizen soldiers who could be called upon in time of war to fight but who held other jobs (or who only served in the army for a couple of years). The Spartans had a standing army who trained constantly. Consequently, they were tough to beat. They worked hard and lived a no-frills life, unlike the cushy Athenians. (Look up the word *spartan* in the dictionary now; you'll find it means "marked by strict self-discipline, frugality, and the avoidance of luxury.") They sent their boys to live in army barracks at the age of seven. And they worked out — fighting and fitness training — constantly.

Helots were Mycenaean slaves that they took over...
There were two classes of people in Sparta. One was the *perioeci*, the soldiers and people who paid taxes and were protected by law. The other

63

FLOCAB SPITS FACTS LIKE AN ALMANAC

Zeus was something special
Of the Greeks' many gods, Zeus was No. 1: a thunderbolt-tossing, lady-loving, always-up-for-a-good-time guy. And his story was pretty special.

Zeus was the son of Cronos, who had swallowed all of his previous children, because he'd heard that one would overtake him. But Zeus's mom, Rhea, tricked Cronos by dressing a rock like a baby, so Cronos swallowed the rock instead. Zeus was then raised by a goat. When Zeus grew up, he made Cronos throw up all the other kids he had swallowed. Zeus fought some Titans and made one of them, Atlas, hold up the sky forever. Zeus had lots of babies with his sister, Hera, and with other gods as well. His favorite child of all, though, was Heracles. Thanks to the Romans, we know this guy as Hercules: The body-building, children-loving, bi-sexual demigod who wrestled Titans and made the world safe for humankind.

were the **Helots,** the serf or slave class. These were the former inhabitants of nearby Messenia. The Spartans conquered it in 640-620 BC and put the Helots to work in Sparta. They had to grow food and do a lot of other work, thereby allowing the Spartans to concentrate on their military activities.

Let's keep it classical and take it back to Athens, where...
Of all the Greek city-states, it was perhaps **Athens** that most influenced the way we think about ancient Greece. The Athenians gave us democracy. The city fostered the arts and letters. It's where the Acropolis and the Parthenon are; it was home to the great writers Socrates and Aeschylus, and the great thinkers Socrates, Aristotle, and Plato. The city has always been admired and loved by Europeans and Americans.

They had the first government with citizens running it...
Early Greeks were very forward-thinking in their politics. They were the first to come up with the concept of **democracy**, where rulers were elected rather installed by force or via inheritance. This concept — democracy, or "government by the people" — was introduced in Athens in about 500 BC. Before that, rule in Athens was by **oligarchy,** which means "government by a few": A handful of aristocrats, or rich noblemen, made all the decisions. But then an aristocrat named Cleisthenes rose to prominence. He was of the opinion that the rich classes in Athens had too much power. He wanted to give the power back to the people. So he and the populace threw out the aristocrats and set up the world's

LYRICS continued

And I'll have some olive branches,
And we'll have a
Party at the Parthenon!

In addition to democracy,
Athens is home
To the fathers of philosophy.
Take Socrates, he asked questions,
To teach his students,
And Plato was the best one.
He was known for his book,
The Republic,
His ideal type of government
Was the subject.
He taught Aristotle
At his own Academy,
And that dude used reason
As a strategy.
The tutor to young Alexander
The Great, who became the
Commander. "Stand up!"
He took Persia, he took Phoenicia,
He took India, Israel, and Egypt.
Meanwhile,
He was spreading Greek style,
Why you think you read *The*
Odyssey now?
It's an epic.
And the Greeks never caught
Half-stepping,
They could be an
Olympic contestant.

Well, all right.
The Minoans and Mycenaeans,
Thanks for the inspiration.
You're invited to the
Party at the Parthenon!

Phnius designed it.
Meet you at the third column,

earliest democracy. Many of the early city-state governments not only allowed people to participate — they expected it. It was almost a requirement that people be involved. Voting residents of Athens were called **citizens**; they were the only ones in society who could own land and hold political office. Back then you had to be over 18 years of age — and male.

Democracy extended by Pericles...
One of the great Athenian rulers was **Pericles** (c. 495-429 BC). Born in the city, Pericles was a champion of democracy. He helped extend it to even more citizens, and he encouraged it in other city-states as well. Many historians believe the golden age of Greek democracy was during Pericles's rule. He helped make Athens the most important city-state - during his time the Parthenon was built, among other great buildings of the Acropolis.

He built the Parthenon, ushered in the Golden Age...
The **Parthenon** was a large temple devoted to Athena, goddess of wisdom and war and protector of Athens. A model of the classical style of architecture, it was surrounded by 46 columns. The building was designed by the sculptor **Phidias**, whose statue of Athena is inside. It remains one of the most famous buildings in the world.

Athens is home to the fathers of philosophy...
The Athenians placed a high value on intellectual development and culture. They made huge achievements in the fields of philosophy, literature, mathematics, and the sciences. Three of the greatest philosophic minds of

all time came from Athens in rapid succession — Socrates, Plato, and Aristotle. At roughly the same time, **Euclid** (c. 300 BC) was revolutionizing mathematics, especially geometry. **Sophocles** wrote great tragedies that would be read for centuries. **Hippocrates** became a great doctor and made many landmark discoveries; the oath that every doctor takes before practicing is named after him. The golden age of Athens was a golden age of the mind.

Take Socrates, he asked questions...

A very famous philosopher, **Socrates** (469-399 BC) was a teacher in Athens. These days, he's best known for committing suicide by drinking hemlock, but in his day his ideas were what got him noticed. Unlike many other philosophers, Socrates didn't write his ideas down; he spread them through conversation. He was famous for his questions. If a student were trying to figure something out, Socrates would ask him questions and make him draw his own conclusions. He taught many famous pupils, but the best known is probably Plato.

To teach his students, and Plato was the best one...

Plato (429-347 BC) is among the most important thinkers - not just in Greek history but in world history. He's perhaps most recognized for his book *The Republic*, in which he describes his idea of the best government. He thought that smart people should run it with fairness and justice (rather than a democracy, which was open to people he considered less wise). Plato opened his own school in a little grove called the **Academy,** which is where that word comes from.

He taught Aristotle at his own Academy...

Aristotle (384-322 BC) was a student of Plato's at his Academy in Athens. Some people consider him the greatest thinker of all in Greece. He was the tutor for Alexander the Great when Alexander was a young kid, and he founded a school in Athens called the **Lyceum** that was in competition with Plato's Academy. Aristotle is famous for his organized manner of thinking. He believed in using logic and reason, a careful thinking process that works like this: If A is true, and A equals B, then B is true. (Those are just the basics.)

LYRICS continued

At the party at the Parthenon!

I hired some lute players to do an Athena tribute tonight, at the Party at the Parthenon!

Once again,
Bring your own Trireme and
I'll see you tonight,
At the party at the Parthenon!

Alexander the Great, who became the commander...
The **Peloponnesian War** took a lot out of the Greeks. The huge battles between the Athenians and the Spartans ravaged much of the territory here, and the men were worn out or dead. **King Philip of Macedon**, a country to the north of Greece, saw this and decided the area was ripe for the taking. He moved in and conquered Greece. His son, Alexander (the Great), took over in 336 BC at the age of 20.

He took Persia, he took Phoenicia...
Alexander became one of the most successful military leaders in world history — and he did it in 13 years. When he assumed power after his father was assassinated, many people thought he was too young and that he'd have a hard time holding on to Greece. Not only did he retain the city-states of Greece, but he added to them much of the rest of the known world. He took over Persia, Phoenicia, Israel and Egypt. He expanded his empire all the way to what is now India and Afghanistan. Alexander was a huge fan of Greek culture and spread it throughout his empire. Of course, Alexander the Great was mostly great at killing people and organizing soldiers to better kill other soldiers.

Meanwhile, he was spreading Greek style...
Greece is a very hilly and mountainous country, which made travel over land hard. So naturally, the Greeks became a talented seagoing people. One of their most famous vessels was the **trireme**, a 100-foot-long warship, powered by as many as 170 oarsmen sitting in three rows. The vessels had

a ram in front to allow rowers to bash into their enemies, and a square sail that could be raised to give them a break when the wind was good.

Why you think you read the Odyssey now? It's an epic...

The Greeks liked their poetry, especially epic poetry. **Epics** were long poems — as lengthy as novels today. They usually told the story of a great hero and his travels. The two most famous epics of ancient Greece were *The Iliad* and *The Odyssey*, both of which were written by the poet Homer, dating back to about 700 BC. *The Iliad* is about the Trojan War, a huge conflict between the Greeks and the people of Troy. *The Odyssey* recounts the adventures of the Greek warrior Odysseus as he struggles to return home from the war and meets all kinds of crazy creatures.

And the Greeks never caught half-stepping...

We may call it mythology today, but to the Greeks themselves, their religion was very real. Before you laugh at how ridiculous it sounds, realize that perhaps future people will view our religions as myths one day.

The Greeks believed in a **pantheon** of gods, which translates to one for just about everything. They had gods for love, gods for celebration, gods for metalworking. They used these deities, who resided atop **Mount Olympus**, to explain all manner of natural phenomena. Thunder and lightning, for example, came from Zeus, king of the gods. The sun shone thanks to Apollo. And, interestingly, they believed that the gods could and did come down from on high and interact with regular people (including making babies with them). Hercules, half man, half god, may be the best-known result of one of these relationships.

They could be an Olympic contestant...

The Greeks celebrated their gods — and heroes — by holding athletic competitions. One such event occurred every four years in the village of Olympia, and it was called the **Olympic Games**. Participants competed in all manner of contests: running, jumping, boxing, throwing. These Olympic Games were held for more than 1,000 years. In 1896 a group of nations from around the world held a new version of the Olympic Games in Athens. And it's these same Olympics that we watch on our TVs every four years today.

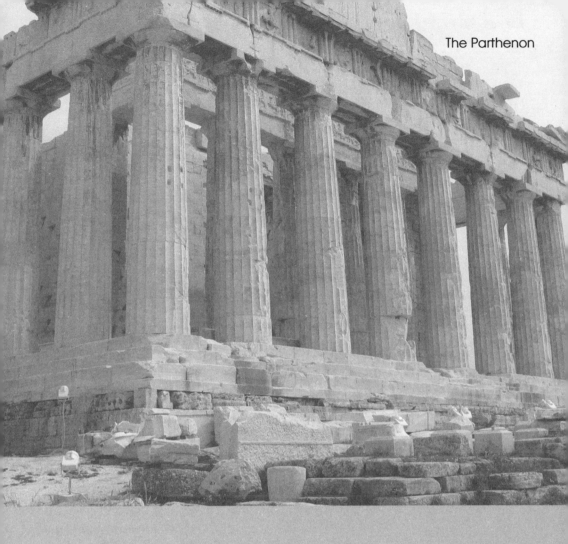

HISTORY SPEAKS

"An unexamined life is not worth living."

– Aristotle

"Poetry comes nearer to vital truth than history."

- Plato

CHAPTER 10:

I AM SPARTACUS

The Roman Republic and Empire: 509 BC to 476 AD

INTRO

They say that the United States of America is a democracy, but technically it isn't. In a **democracy**, all people vote on all the laws. America is actually a **republic**: We vote for people (senators and representatives) and *they* vote on the laws. This means we have more time to work, take naps and chat online. But where did this amazing idea of a republic come from? It came from the Romans (who adapted it from the Greeks).

Life in the **Roman Republic** wasn't all good, though. Like many other civilizations at the time, the Romans had slaves - lots of them. One slave, a man named Spartacus, led one of the largest slave uprisings in the history of the world. It was so big, the Romans called it a war. And indeed, that's what it was.

A Gladiator

I AM SPARTACUS

LYRICS

They call me Spartacus,
I was a normal guy
Until the Romans invaded;
I watched my mama die.
She didn't get a grave,
They killed my father too,
They made me a slave
And told me what to do.
Made me a gladiator,
They threw me in the ring, and
I fought some lions and soldiers,
I'm fighting everything.
They make you kill a man,
They make you kill again,
I killed a guy, took his helmet off;
It was my friend.
I said, this needs to end,
I mean I'm getting close,
I'm like Vesuvius, baby,
I mean I'm set to blow.
The Roman Republic got rich
Off of slave's backs,
So now I think we need
Some payback.
Me and 69 guys
Snuck into the kitchen,
Got 69 knives,
This was the beginning
Of the uprising,
And we escaped our cells,
Spread the word to other slaves:
You can escape as well.
And they flocked to me;
See, they wanted to see
What life's like
When you "give us, us free."
Like Julius Caesar,

CONTEXT AND BACKGROUND

During its early years, Rome was governed by kings, like everywhere else at the time. One of these kings was an evil man who had many of his people killed. He was eventually overthrown by a group of men from the noble class. In 509 BC, they decided that, rather than have kings as they always had, they'd establish a form of government similar to the one they saw the Greeks using. Thus began the famous Roman Republic.

They call me Spartacus, I was normal guy…
Imagine that you are a farmer's son, somewhere near Greece. You help your family plant crops, you have a crush on the girl down the road, and you hate it when your mom yells at you. But as you grow up, a kingdom grows in Rome. Eventually it will become a powerful republic, and then an unstoppable empire. When their armies march through your town to conquer your land and make your family pay taxes, some people in your village, like your dad, fight back. But the Roman army is hard to beat. They kill your father and take many of the other villagers captive, including you. You are a young boy, who looks like he might grow to be a strong warrior. The year is about 100 years before Jesus was born. Your name is Spartacus.

Until the Romans invaded; I watched my mama die…
The Romans were a hard-thinking, but aggressive bunch. Their main rival was not the farmers of Greece, but a powerful city-state in northern Africa

called **Carthage**. In 274 BC, the people of Carthage were afraid the Romans were going to attack them. So they decided to attack Rome first. This led to the first **Punic War**. The Romans and the Carthaginians fought for control of the island of Sicily. The Romans eventually won, but the two mighty cultures would fight again in 218 and 146 BC during the Second and Third Punic Wars. These were again turf battles, for control of Spain, for Greece and even for Carthage itself. During the Second War, a great Carthaginian general named **Hannibal** rode through the mountains into Italy on herds of war elephants! But every time the Romans won a battle, they took over more and more of Europe. They eventually went to Carthage and wrecked the place, driving all its people out and burning it to the ground.

She didn't get a grave, they killed my father too...

As Rome expanded, Romans became more and more proud of their interesting government. At the top of the republic were two **consuls** - sort of like co-presidents. They both had to agree on which course of action to take - one could *veto* (the Latin word for "I forbid it,") the idea of the other. Beneath them was the **Senate**, a group of elected men from the ranks of the wealthy, (and they were all men — women weren't allowed to be in the Senate or be consuls). Senators served for life, and they helped the consuls decide what was best for Rome. Sometimes they took advice from the **tribunes**, who were men elected to speak for the poorer classes. The tribunes got their power from the **Assembly**, which was a huge body designed to represent the regular

people and working classes. Tribunes could veto laws in the Senate, so they were positions of some note.

They made me a slave and told me what to do...

Starting a republic was another huge step forward for the civilized world. But in its early days with this new form of government, Rome was by no means an open, free-thinking, democratic place. First, the only people who could be elected were the **patricians**, or nobles. The **plebeians**, or common people, were pretty much powerless, not to mention all of the slaves, who had no power whatsoever and were treated terribly. The number of slaves in the Republic grew to hundreds of thousands, maybe even millions. Slaves were so cheap that even a poor farmer could own one.

Made me a gladiator, they threw me in the ring, and...

Ever seen the TV show *American Gladiators*? Two guys and two girls compete in a complex obstacle course, while being challenged by spandex-wearing bodybuilders with names like Laser and Turbo. In the end, everyone smiles and then they cut to a commercial for Xbox or fabric softener.

Things were different for Roman **gladiators**. At the end of one of their matches, one person would survive, and the other would be dead in the sand. These were brutal, savage fights, all done for the amusement of the cheering Roman crowds. The fighters themselves were usually slaves who were forced to fight against their will. The Romans gave them swords, spears, and all kinds of exotic weapons, and dressed them up like foreign soldiers. These were popular matches,

LYRICS continued

I led a whole movement,
We had a 120,000 humans!

*You want to know
Who Spartacus is?
You want to know Spartacus,
I'm Spartacus.*

Now the senators started getting
Scared in Rome,
Cuz we were plundering land near
Their summer homes.
We were fearless; I was like,
Send your best generals,
Send me your
Pompeiis and Caesars.
I'm not a DJ, this hit's not the remix,
We started this like
Romulus and Remus.
"Slaves, join us
If you've had enough,"
We moved on like water
Through an aqueduct.
So you can pray to Jupiter,
You can pray to Mars,
You'll need more than gods,
You'll be seeing stars.
Now Rome had a problem,
I'm Spartacus,
And we fight to the death
If you're harming us.
But I didn't want this;
I wanted peace, I wanted Pax,
I wanted to be clean
Like a public bath.
I want to walk with my daughter
Through Rome,
In the Forum,
Maybe hear a speech,
In the Colosseum, see a show.
But Roman legions came,

held in cities throughout the Republic. As many as 50,000 people would fill the Roman Colosseum for gladiator fights; they'd spend the whole day watching contest after contest. A lot of blood was spilled. Was Roman civilization really so civilized?

I said, this needs to end, I mean I'm getting close…
In the Roman Republic, being free really meant something. And that made it all the harder to be a slave.
Like other early societies, the Romans had a series of laws that people had to follow. And for the first time, these laws were not just the same old ones like "you can't steal," and "you can't kill." They also included laws that protected people's basic rights to be free. Back then, that was unheard of, and it set the stage for many of the human rights laws we enjoy today. They included things like a right to be present at one's own trial; the right to not be killed before you're convicted; the right to be judged fairly; the right of plebeians to be treated fairly by patricians. This was truly groundbreaking stuff. Basically, these laws came about because the patrician class (the wealthy) often tried to take advantage of the plebeian class (the poor). In 494 BC the plebeians threatened to leave the empire - there would go all the servants and cleaning people and army! The patricians therefore compromised and gave them these **Twelve Tables of Law**.

I'm like Vesuvius, baby, I mean I'm set to blow…
Mount Vesuvius showed little mercy. When it erupted on August 24, 79 AD, it shot ash and gas more than 12

FLOCAB SPITS FACTS LIKE AN ALMANAC

There is no doubt that Roman culture has influenced the modern world and made a lot of wonderful contributions. Our literature, poetry, architecture and government owe a large thanks to the Romans. But many history books don't mention Rome's dark side: The reason that the Roman Empire was so big and mighty was that the Romans were the most ruthless and skilled murderers in the area.

When the Roman armies conquered a town, they would often kill every living soul in that town: men, women, children, even dogs and other animals. They did this for the same reason that a terrorist sets off a bomb: to make people afraid. So the Romans terrorized Europe to build their empire.

Does that mean that we should call them terrorists?

miles up into the air, and in one day it buried the nearby town of **Pompeii** under almost 20 feet of ash and rock. The people of this city south of Rome had no warning — and no time to escape. Many did get out in time, but the whole city was wiped out. It was a horrible tragedy, but it left an almost perfectly preserved Roman city for historians to study. Archaeologists learned much about early Roman history from digging through the ruins of Pompeii. Time simply stopped for the people of Pompeii that day. Historians even found bread still in the oven and gladiators chained up!

Me and 69 guys, snuck into the kitchen...
Spartacus and 69 other slaves were held in a gladiator training school in Capua, near Naples. The land around Naples was beautiful, so many rich Romans had built summer homes on the hills. They could get tasty oysters from the nearby bay, and a local man even specialized in building heated swimming pools. So when Spartacus and his men took knives from the cook's shop and broke out of their "school," they had lots of rich estates to rob. They took metal from their chains and shackles and melted it down to make weapons. Because they were messing with the homes of the rich and famous, the Romans sent a large army to destroy the slaves, even though there were only 70 of them.

Of the uprising, and we escaped our cells...
Spartacus and his men decided to camp on the side of Mount Vesuvius. This was 150 years before it would erupt, so it was still safe. Three

LYRICS continued

And yes, they are well-trained,
I'd rather die free
Then live like a slave.
I'll beat them back,
I said, I'll beat them back,
I'm free now,
And I'll never go back!

thousand Roman soldiers marched to the base of the mountain, trapping the slaves, but Spartacus and his men knew about escaping from tight situations. They tied vines together and rappelled down the steep cliffs on the far side, then snuck up on the soldiers from behind. The 3,000 sleeping soldiers didn't stand a chance: Spartacus and his men routed them.

Like Julius Caesar I led a whole movement...

The Republic was already weakened by generals who had grabbed more power than the constitution allowed. But one man took it further, claiming that he was the "dictator for life." This was Julius Caesar.

Julius Caesar (100-44 BC) made his name as a general in the fields of what is now France as well as Britain and parts of Asia. He was elected to the Senate and became consul, a president of sorts. But Caesar wanted more and more power for himself. When he declared himself "dictator for life," many members of the Senate began to worry about Rome going from a democracy to a dictatorship (which it would anyway soon enough). A large conspiracy to have him killed was formed, and he was stabbed by a group of 60 men, including at least one he considered a friend. This brought about the famous line, *Et tu Brute?*, which means, "Even you, Brutus?" Many leaders after him took the name of Caesar to borrow some of his popularity with the people. The month of July is named after Julius Caesar.

We had 120,000 humans...

Many people were not happy that Julius Caesar turned the government away from the republic ideal and back toward a monarchy - including the famous philosopher **Cicero** (c. 106-43 BC). You could say he was the best emcee of his day, a popular speaker who could really excite the crowd. He gave many talks about the need to restore the Senate to prominence and wanted checks in place to stop the power-grab of the generals.

After Julius Caesar was assassinated, his cousin **Mark Antony** looked sure to take over. He was well known for his relationship with his wife, the Egyptian queen **Cleopatra**. But the powerful pair had an even more powerful rival — Julius's adopted son, **Octavian**, soon to be known as Augustus. He defeated Mark Antony and Cleopatra in 31 BC in a battle at Actium, off the coast of Greece.

Now the senators started getting scared in Rome...

Like Julius, **Augustus Caesar** (63 BC-14 AD) has a month named after him. (Guess which one?) And just like his father, he was one of the most powerful leaders in the history of the **Roman Empire**. After defeating Antony and Cleopatra, Octavian emerged as the sole ruler of Rome. Until then, the Roman Republic usually had at least two consuls at the top. Now there was just Octavian. He changed his name to Augustus, which meant "exalted one," and he was quick to consolidate power to eventually become the first Roman emperor, putting an end to republican rule.

Send me your Pompeiis, and Caesars...

Nero was the fifth Roman emperor. He came to power amid a lot of ugliness, which continued through his reign. His mother poisoned the previous emperor so that he'd take the throne. Then **Nero** (37-68 AD) poisoned another rival and, not long afterward, had his mom killed, too. Not a nice fellow - or a particularly good emperor, as his reign was characterized by all of the mistakes he made. He was blamed for a great fire that consumed much of Rome in 64 AD. Nero, in turn, blamed the small Christian sect and saw that they were persecuted for it. Meanwhile, revolts and rebellions were underway throughout his empire, and he couldn't seem to do much about them. He ended up committing suicide.

We started this like Romulus and Remus...

Many countries have a founding legend, and Rome is no exception. According to Rome's legend, a pair of twins, Romulus and Remus, were found floating down the Tiber River in a basket. A wolf pulled them out of the water and raised them as her own boys. Later, the twins decided to build a city on the spot where they had been found. During the construction process, however, they argued, and Romulus ended up killing Remus. He then named the city after himself.

We moved on like water through an aqueduct...

The Romans understood the importance of moving water, just like the Egyptians and the Mesopotamians before them. They devised a clever system of troughs through which their water supply could flow. Many of these **aqueducts** started in the ground, but by the time they reached the city, they traveled up over arches built on big columns. These were huge stone gutters that carried water all across the city. They were truly large — bigger than buildings - and most were wide enough (often three feet) for workers to walk through. The 11 major aqueducts were marvels of engineering; the longest brought water for more than 59 miles. Some were located in other countries, like France, which were occupied by the Romans. Many can still be seen around Rome today.

So pray to Jupiter, and you can pray to Mars ...

Today, Rome is closely affiliated with the Catholic Church. But in ancient times, it was a place of many gods. The early Romans borrowed a whole set of holy figures from the Greeks.

This group of deities — called the pantheon — was pretty much the same in both places; the Romans just gave them different names. Zeus, the king of the gods, became Jupiter. Athena the warrior became Minerva. Aries, the god of war, became Mars. You get the idea. All of our planets are named after Roman gods.

Everyday people had gods for their households, and people spent a lot of time praying. Besides Greece, ancient Roman religions were influenced by many of the places they conquered, and the Romans were usually good about allowing people to continue worshipping however they wanted, as long as they caused no problems with the empire. They killed Jesus for fear that he might lead a

rebellion.

But I didn't want this; I wanted peace, I wanted Pax...

Throughout much of ancient history, warfare was the norm. But it wasn't always that way. From about 20 BC to 180 AD, there was a peaceful period in the Roman Empire during which people just lived, more or less happily. There were no large wars or battles, and trade occurred with people as far away as China, Spain, Britain, Egypt, and what is now Scandinavia. This time period was called the **Pax Romana** (Roman peace), and the quality of life was high for many of the empire's citizens.

I wanted to be clean like a public bath...

The Romans were a clean people - meaning they liked to bathe. (Not everyone did, back then.) Most Romans didn't have hot water in their homes, so they went to public bathhouses. They built at least one in each town. They were usually tile-lined places with swimming pools, steam rooms, and spaces for exercising or playing games. Romans used all sorts of rubs and ointments to treat their skin, like olive oil and pumice powder. Then it was time to put the toga back on.

In the Forum, maybe hear a speech...

Like any city, Rome had a downtown - a square called the **Forum**. This was where the Romans would go to do their shopping, banking, and even to eat out. Many of the major buildings of government were here, and because the Forum was always so busy with people, it became known as a place where speeches were given.

In the Colosseum, see a show...

Just like we have stadiums today, the Romans had their **Colosseum**. The massive, almost-circular structure had room for 55,000 spectators to sit and watch gladiator or other entertainers. Huge sections of the Colosseum still survive to this day; it's a popular tourist attraction in Rome.

But the Roman legions came, and yes, they are well trained...

Christianity owes a large debt to **Constantine** (c. 285-337 AD). He was the first emperor to believe in the faith. Previously, Christians had been persecuted by the Romans, who sometimes even fed them to the lions at sporting events. The emperor Constantine changed all that, adopting the **Christian** faith himself and spreading it far and wide. He relocated his capital to what is now Turkey, and called it "New Rome," and named the city **Constantinople**.

I'm free now, and I'll never go back...

Unfortunately, the uprising of Spartacus and his fellow slaves didn't end slavery in Rome. Spartacus and his army were defeated in 70 BC, but he served as a role model for future revolutionaries like Karl Marx and Che Guevara.

HISTORY SPEAKS

"Veni, vidi, vici." (I came, I saw, I conquered.)

– Julius Caesar

"The die is cast."

– Julius Caesar, when crossing the Rubicon, and deciding to march on Rome

CHAPTER 11:

GETTIN' BYZZY WITH IT

The Byzantine Empire: 395 to 1453

INTRO

When the Roman Empire split apart, the biggest chunk was a large territory in the east. This land was ruled out of Constantinople, a beautiful city where Europe meets Asia. The empire later became known as the Byzantine Empire, and it became a powerful player in the region. Any country where a poor actress, the daughter of a bear trainer, can grow up to be Empress must be a cool place.

Empress Theodora

LYRICS

America's hot dogs, baseball,
And Barney,
Bad health care,
But a strong army.
The Romans felt the same way
We feel today,
Like Frosted Flakes: We're great.
We're No. 1,
Like the top of the charts,
But then the Roman Empire
Split apart.
The land in the west
Cut up into fiefs,
But the Empire in the east
Stayed tight.
It's the Byzantine Empire, surely,
We're rocking Asia Minor,
Now it's Turkey?
The capital was Constantinople,
Now it's Istanbul,
Not Constantinople.
"Ding."
Justinian steps into the ring,
Conquering lands like
It was his thing.
He fell in love with this girl,
Theodora, the actress doing
Backflips knew tactics.
She changed the laws,
She's keeping it wise,
'Cause now men can't
Just be beating their wives.
When a rebellion rose,
Justin wanted to go,
But Theodora said,
"Nah, we can't go,
We need to stay and fight."
And that day she's right,

CONTEXT AND BACKGROUND

The Romans felt the same way we feel today...
We have a very high standard of living in America today. People from all kinds of countries risk their lives just to get into America to live and work. We build mighty cities and fast cars; we create music and movies that the rest of the world loves. But will it always be that way?

We're No. 1, like the top of the charts...
Around 110 AD, the Romans were likewise on top of the world. They controlled most of Europe, the northern coast of Africa, the Nile, and the Middle East around the Mediterranean. Peace within the empire meant that people could relax and not worry too much about an army rolling through to destroy their town. Rich people could sit in their heated swimming pools, and have slaves feed them grapes and read them the hottest new poetry. Some must have figured that the good times would never end.

But then the Roman Empire split apart...
But by the 400s, the Roman Empire was falling apart. Tribes of Germanic invaders had moved into what is now Italy and crowded everyone else out. The Roman Empire had basically split by this point into western and eastern halves. The Roman **Emperor Diocletian** thought it was too big for one person to rule, so he gave territory in the east to a co-emperor in 286 AD. The Eastern Roman Empire became the **Byzantine Empire**. It flourished for 1,000 years

after its counterpart in the west fell.

The land in the west cut up into fiefs, but the Empire in the east stayed tight...

While the land in the west was divided into fiefs ruled by king-warlords, the Byzantine Empire continued to expand. It centered on the old city of Byzantium, which we now know as **Istanbul**, Turkey. During the Byzantine Empire it was called **Constantinople**.

It's the Byzantine Empire, surely...

The Byzantine Empire was inspired not only by Rome, but by the Greeks as well. This part of the world was once a Greek outpost. The ancient city of Byzantium was Greek, and the people here spoke Greek rather than Roman Latin (though they still considered themselves Romans). The **Emperor Constantine** was an avowed fan of Greco-Roman culture. Much of what we know about the Greeks and Romans comes from this time because monks under Constantine copied old books to save them. Constantine was also a Christian and promoted his faith whenever he could.

The capital was Constantinople...

Renamed after the emperor Constantine, Constantinople sat on the Bosporus, a narrow stretch of land between the Black Sea to the north and the Mediterranean Sea to the south. The Roman emperor Constantine had made it the seat of his power in 330 AD. By the time the western Roman Empire collapsed, Constantinople was one of the world's most important cities — the largest in the world during the Middle Ages that would follow. In many ways it gave old Rome a run for its money. The city sat at the point where Europe and Asia met, and as such was in the perfect position to benefit from trade between the two. By the standards of the day, the city was wealthy — even richer than Rome. People were literate. There were libraries and stadiums, gardens and palaces. Many citizens dressed in silk rather than the rawhide everyone else wore. It was an impressive place.

Now it's Istanbul, not Constantinople...

Constantinople is now Istanbul because in 1453 the **Ottoman Turks** overran the city and put an end to the Byzantine Empire. Constantinople had been weakened during the Crusades and its battles with the Serbians and Bulgarians. It wasn't very stable by 1453, so the Turks used modern artillery to take it over.

FLOCAB SPITS FACTS LIKE AN ALMANAC

One source of information on Theodora is a Byzantine scholar named Procopius. Procopius wasn't exactly a fan of Theodora; in his writings he describes her with some harsh language. Calling her the "most depraved of all courtesans," he accuses her of bewitching Justinian and torturing her enemies in ways that can't be described on these pages.

LYRICS continued

Because Justinian defeated
Them that night.
Pit foe against foe,
Your foes will be weak,
That's the Byzantine trick just for
Keeping the peace.

We get busy with it,
Y'all get dizzy with it.
Don't question, we're the best,
Where the East meets West.

We get busy with it,
Y'all get dizzy with it.
Byzantine stay busy,
We rock, rock the city, what!

Now it seems we Byzantines
Practice Christianity seven days
A week, at least.
We pray to icons,
Little pictures of Mary, Jesus,
And some of the saints.
But some leaders said,
"Uh-uh, you can't,"
Cuz the second commandment
Says don't pray to paint.
If you score three goals,
That's a hat trick,
But this controversy
Was iconoclastic.
When Leo III said "no" to icons,
We still had 'em,
So now we have to hide 'em.
The Pope in Rome said
Icons were just fine,
And it's heresy if you say otherwise.
Said, "If you do I'll hate you,
I'll excommunicate you,
Kick you out the Church, and
Send you back to grade school."

"Ding." Justinian steps into the ring...
Back when Byzantine was nearing its
height of power, **Justinian** (483-565)
became emperor. He was another
fan of the Greeks and Romans and
did much to restore the grandeur of
old Rome. He took back many of the
lands that the Roman Empire had
lost in Italy, Africa, and Spain. He also
had his scholars dig up the old laws of
Rome, the Twelve Tables; made sure
that there were no unchristian rules
among them, and added his own laws
to them. What resulted was called the
Justinian Code. It was an important
document in that it officially granted
people under his rule a new set of civil
rights, and paved the way for later
documents like the Magna Carta and
the Bill of Rights.

He fell in love with this girl, Theodora...
Justinian's wife was **Theodora** (c.500-
548). She was a perfect example of
the old saying that behind every great
man was a great woman. Amazingly,
Theodora wasn't born a noble
- she was the daughter of a circus
bear-trainer. She joined the family
business, working on stage in goofy
and sometimes scandalous comedy
shows, and as a courtesan, captured
the heart of Justinian just before he
became emperor. He had to change
the laws to marry her, because until
then, an emperor couldn't marry an
actress.

**'Cause now men can't just be beating
their wives...**
Theodora more or less ruled alongside
Justinian; she was considered the
Empress. She was a very influential
figure in a number of ways. She
encouraged her husband to pass laws
that were favorable to women and

promoted women's rights, including making it illegal for husbands to beat their wives.

When a rebellion rose, Justin wanted to go...

Theodora is probably most famous for stepping up when Justinian wanted to run and hide following the uprising in Constantinople in 532. Theodora convinced him to stay and fight. They overcame the rebels and rebuilt the city, which had been badly damaged. One of the buildings they had built was the **Hagia Sophia**, Church of the Holy Wisdom. One of the architectural wonders of the world, it still stands in Istanbul today.

Now, it seems we Byzantines practice Christianity...

The people of the Byzantine Empire were extremely religious. They were Christians, and their faith can be seen in their architecture, literature and art.

One art form that flourished during the Byzantine Empire was **mosaic art**. Made from small tiles of ceramic or glass, these pictures were similar to those the Romans made, but the Byzantines took mosaics to a new level. In Constantinople, it was common to cover walls and ceilings with them. They were often made with a type of glass that sparkled or reflected light, and they typically depicted Christian scenes. Some art scholars consider Byzantine mosaics among the finest examples of the art.

We pray to icons, little pictures of Mary, Jesus and some of the saints...

The people of Constantinople combined religion and art in mosaics, as well as in paintings known as **icons**.

Icons were portraits of important figures within the Church, from Jesus to the saints. Often painted with slightly elongated faces against a gold background, icons became very important in the Church. Many people in the empire considered icons windows into heaven, and believed they offered a direct connection to the person pictured. People who prayed to these images even claimed that they granted miracles.

The second commandment says don't pray to paint...

Some important Church leaders weren't fans of icons, though. They thought that praying to an icon was a violation of the second Commandment, which says not to worship images of God. These people were called **iconoclasts**, and the battle over icons became known as the **iconoclastic controversy**. Since Christianity was so important in the empire, this issue quickly became a huge deal.

The Pope in Rome said icons were just fine...

In 726, Byzantine **Emperor Leo III** outlawed the worship of icons. This really stirred things up, because the Pope thought icons were fine. The pope was (and still is) the leader of the Catholic Church, ruling from Rome. He wanted to allow icons because most people in Europe couldn't read; he thought icons helped them connect with their faith.

So the Pope declared opposition to icons to be a **heresy**, something that went against Church doctrine. Saying or doing something that is a heresy made you a **heretic**. This was no small thing; at various times in history, people have been killed and

LYRICS continued

In 1054,
The Church split in two parts:
Roman Catholic
And Eastern Orthodox.

Hook

tortured for being a heretic.

If you do I'll hate you, I'll excommunicate you...
But the Pope wasn't about to kill or torture anyone. Instead, he threatened iconoclasts with **excommunication** - when the Church doesn't allow you to be a member anymore.

In 1054, Church split up in two parts: Roman Catholic and Eastern Orthodox...
The iconoclastic controversy added to the tension between the Church leaders in Constantinople and Rome. The two cities were far apart and culturally different, which lead to many disagreements about how things should be run. Finally in 1054, things reached the breaking point. In what's known as the **Great Schism,** the Christian Church split in half: In the West it was the Roman Catholic Church, and in the East, the **Eastern Orthodox Church**. The two churches remain separate to this day.

Byzantine Icon

CHAPTER 12:

MIDDLE AGES: EUROPE

432 to 1500

INTRO

The thousand years between the fall of the Roman Empire in the fifth century to the Renaissance in the 16th century is known as the Middle Ages – the era of knights and kings, Crusades and Vikings, castles and catapults, and stories of King Arthur, Robin Hood, and Ivanhoe. It all existed within a feudal (FYOO-dal) government system, set up to protect villagers from invading tribes.

It worked like this: The king would give a large portion of land — called a fief — to a duke, who would look after it for him. The duke would swear fealty (loyalty) to the king and send knights to help him at times of war. He'd have farmers work the land and send food. The duke would divide up his lands among his counts, barons or earls, who would in turn pledge their allegiance to both the duke and the king. And they too would send their soldiers. It was a pyramid scheme of sorts that enabled a king to control his subjects.

LYRICS

I'm on a crusade for Christendom,
The holy cross on my neck like floss,
Steel sword and a black horse.
It's 1095 AD,
The Byzantine Empire is in need,
Alexius is calling me
Like I'm his last hope;
Urban II is Pope.
I cross foreign lands
With dust in my throat,
Thus began the war,
200 years or more,
Straight thuggin' between the
Christians and Muslims.
I'm led by Richard I,
The lion hearted,
In a fight against Saladin
And all of his men.
With legends like
Robin Hood and Ivanhoe,
One king finally crowned,
Now the cities can grow.

We tell a story that's
Right from the pages,
Talk about Europe,
Talk about the Middle Ages.
In dark times,
We knights are the bravest,
Crusades and plagues,
It's dangerous.

Now you're a serf,
But the surf's never up,
You're working in the fields,
But you're covered in mud.
You're not slave,

CONTEXT AND BACKGROUND

I'm on a crusade for Christendom...
One of the most powerful forces in
Europe during the Middle Ages was
the Catholic Church. In many ways it
united various nation states even when
they otherwise did not get along.
The large and undefined region they
all occupied was not called Europe
back then, but **"Christendom"** or the
community of Christians.

1095 AD the Byzantine Empire is in
need...
In 1095 AD, **Byzantine Emperor Alexius**
sent out word that he needed help
holding off the invading Turks. The
Pope at the time, **Urban II**, made a
famous proclamation in Clermont
France. He told all Christian soldiers
they should join in the fight and go to
Alexius's aid. Armies of knights from
across Europe made their way east
toward Jerusalem, wearing crosses
over their armor. Thus began the **First
Crusade**.

Thus began the war, 200 years or
more...
There wasn't just one holy war, but
a series of Crusades over a period
of 200 years. In each, the Christian
European forces fought the Muslim
Turks for control of the Holy Land. The
Third Crusade pitted two of the most
famous and brilliant men of the time
against one another - **Richard I** of
England and **Saladin** of Egypt and
Syria.

I'm led by Richard I, the lion hearted...
The son of Henry II of England, Richard
(1157-1199) was a popular king who

87

went off to fight in the Crusades. While he was away, he put his brother, Prince John into power, setting off a chain of events. King Richard spent only six months of his 10 year reign as king in England (he thought it was rainy and gloomy there); the rest of the time he was off fighting for the Holy Land or resided on his fabulous estates in France. He was written into English folklore as the good king in the story of Robin Hood.

One king finally crowned, now the cities can grow...

Feudalism began to decline after the Crusades. Because of the development of cities and economies, kings could just hire the armies they needed. They didn't have to worry about the vassal system — exchanging land for military service. Europe was transitioning toward a money-based economy and away from one based on agriculture.

During the early Middle Ages, there was no such thing as Germany, Spain or Ireland. Instead, kingdoms and fiefdoms were spread out all over the place. Some kings were more powerful than others and began to consolidate their power, making alliances and taking over territory. Out of all this emerged the nation-state, a sovereign power usually run by a single king. By the end of the Middle Ages, the nations of France, England and Spain had emerged beneath royal monarchies.

It's dangerous...

The great era of Roman rule came to an end thanks to tribes of Germanic people from the north. The Romans called them barbarians, their way of saying "people who don't speak like us." Two examples of these "barbarians" were the Goths and the Vandals. The **Goths** were from what is now the eastern part of Germany. In the third century, weak leaders controlled the Roman Empire, which was reeling from fights with the Persians.

The Goths saw this as an opportunity. They wanted territory near them along the Danube River, then held by the Romans. And so they took it, defeating the Roman army at the site. Emboldened by this success, they began to raid farther and farther into Roman territory. They ultimately sacked the city of Rome itself in 410. The **Vandals**, likewise, attacked the Romans about 270. They, too, were after territory and power. The Romans didn't like them, which is why someone who spray-paints today is accused of *vandalism.*

Now you're a serf but the surf's never up...

If anyone really had it rough in the Middle Ages, though, it was the **serf**. He or she was bound to their lord for life. It wasn't exactly slavery, but it was pretty close. The serf wasn't allowed to leave the manor without permission from the lord, and couldn't marry or do much of anything unless the lord gave his blessing. The only good thing about being a serf was that if they could escape, make it to a town, and live there for a year and a day without getting caught, they were free.

You pay those high taxes to your lord, and he protects you from invading hordes...

The **peasants** were the working class under feudalism. They usually were the ones who did the farming, though

LYRICS continued

But you can't leave,
Need permission, like
"Excuse me, could I take a walk
Down the street?"
You pay those high taxes
To your lord,
And he protects you from
linvading hordes.
Knights fight from on horses,
Ride when their lord orders,
Own land, the strongest forces.
The king does whatever he wants,
He's a jerk,
You need a Magna Carta,
"That might work!"
But get set for the men
From the North,
Vikings in longboats with oars.
And there's the No. 1 killer,
That's Attila the Hun,
Marching from the East,
So get ready to run.
But even Charlemagne
Can't save your hide,
When the plague rages,
You're gonna die.

some were servants. Usually, they didn't own their own land, so they had to pay a certain percentage of their income to the person who did own it, like paying rent. This was usually most of what they made, so they stayed very poor.

In exchange for protection from the local noblemen, they were obliged to be foot soldiers in times of war. Even if they owned their own farm, they still had to pay the powerful for protection against thieves and invaders. Though they were free, peasants lived a hardscrabble life of work and toil and were often taken advantage of by the "noble" classes.

Knights fight from on horses, ride when their lord orders…

The men of the noble were often the **knights**. One of the nice things about being a knight was that if you went into battle — and there was always a war going on somewhere – you got to wear armor and ride a horse. Being up high and protected gave you a huge advantage over foot soldiers; you could ride right over them. No wonder everyone wanted to be a knight!

Knights were **vassals** — that is, they promised to lend their military might to a duke or baron in exchange for large tracts of land. They practiced their craft — fighting with swords, axes, and lances — constantly. When there was no battle to be fought, they would often compete in contests to show who was best. They lived by a code of honor called **chivalry**, which was based on courage, loyalty, and kind treatment of others — usually noblewomen. There's a common misconception that knights couldn't move around in their armor and had to be hoisted into the saddle. This

FLOCAB SPITS FACTS LIKE AN ALMANAC

If we all came from Ethiopia hundreds of thousands of years ago, then we're all one people. So why are white people light-skinned and black people dark-skinned? The answer, mostly, is vitamins.

All people originally had brown skin, most likely. Some humans decided to move north, where there was food, but the climate was colder, with shorter days and less sunlight. The people with dark skin started dying faster than those with light skin, because people with light skin were able to soak up vitamin D better. Meanwhile, some people stuck around Ethiopia or moved south. Among these people, the light-skinned people started dying faster, because dark skin was better equipped to handle the sun's rays. Genetically speaking, these are tiny, tiny differences.

wasn't true. They couldn't exactly skip, but they were plenty mobile. In the scheme of things, they had a pretty nice life. Until another knight began hacking at them.

The strongest forces...
Before you could become a knight, you had to help a knight. **Squires** were the young sons of noblemen who apprenticed themselves to a knight. This helped them learn how to fight and understand the ways of chivalry. In exchange for being taught, squires performed tasks for the knights: They served them meals, polished their armor, helped them suit up for battle (it's impossible to put on your own armor), and even followed them off to war. If they performed all these tasks well, they'd be knighted themselves at about the age of 21.

Pages were the little brothers of the squires. They served in various capacities at the court of a knight or king, running errands and bringing messages. They learned manners, how to read and write, how to ride a horse, and began to study swordsmanship. At age 13 the page graduated to life as a squire.

You need a Magna Carta...
King John will always be known for two things. He was the villain against whom Robin Hood and his merry men fought, and he was the king who approved the **Magna Carta** ("Great Charter"). This document was a huge step forward for Western civilization. By stamping it with his seal, King John essentially agreed that he was subject to the law of the land, just like everyone else - Kings would no longer be all-powerful. The Magna Carta granted the people of England many basic human rights. (Of course, most of these were still slanted toward the wealthy.) King John did not want to sign it, but he was forced to by many of his noblemen. When the American colonists were putting their political ideas on paper, they were inspired by older documents like the Magna Carta.

But get set for the men from the North, Vikings in longboats with oars...

In the early days, Europe was an **agrarian** society — life revolved around farming. Somewhere around 500-600 AD, people from what is now Scandinavia — particularly Norway, Denmark, and Sweden — felt like they were running out of land for their crops. Great seamen, they hopped in their boats and went off exploring, searching for more territory. These were the **Vikings,** who traveled by sea in famous longships, narrow vessels with dragonheads at the bow. They would pull up in their boats and raid villages all over what is now Britain, Ireland, France, even as far away as Morocco. They'd take whatever they wanted from the locals, kill those who resisted, and make settlements. They mixed with the French, for example, and became the Normans. They merged with the Slavic people of Eastern Europe and became Russians. Known as the **Norsemen** — or men of the north — the Vikings would make it to North America, long before Columbus did. But they didn't see anything too amazing, and turned around, forgetting about this new world.

And there's the No. 1 killer, that's Attila the Hun...

The **Huns** were another group of invaders. A horse-riding people from Mongolia, they moved to an area along the Danube River in the 270s. They then pushed west, fighting the Goths. The Huns were led by a very powerful leader named Attila (406-453), who caused fear everywhere he went. The Romans were terrified of him; even the barbarians were scared. Attila raided all across Europe, but he was afraid to go to Rome itself because he heard that Italy was infected with disease.

But even Charlemagne can't save your hide...

Charles the Great, more often known as Charlemagne (768-814), was another powerful ruler with an interest in Rome. A masterful military strategist, he built an empire in what is now France and expanded it to include parts of Spain, Germany, and, most important, Italy. **Charlemagne** built the largest kingdom Europe had seen since the Roman Empire - in fact, he proclaimed himself Roman Emperor. (This was 300 years after the Roman Empire fell to pieces.) He was a devout Christian, and his rule brought together many elements of European civilization that had been separate before — Rome, Christianity, and Germanic and Frank tribes.

When the plague rages, you're gonna die...

The **bubonic plague** (a.k.a. the "Black Death") descended upon Europe in the 1300s. A horrible illness that made its way west from Central Asia along trade routes, the disease caused black spots to appear on the body. It killed most people who contracted it - about a third of everyone in Europe at the time. It spread quickly because of poor hygiene and the lack of good food. Many people thought it was a punishment sent by God.

CHAPTER 13:
MIDDLE AGES: ASIA

900 to 1300

INTRO

Humans went from living a nomadic lifestyle to settling down in towns and villages. In general, this made things easier. But some people throughout time had decided it was better to keep moving. So while the Japanese had firmly settled in the villages dotting their island, the **Mongols** of Central Asia kept moving from place to place. **Genghis Khan,** the impressive Mongolian leader, rose to power by exploiting his mobility. If you lived in a town, he could come and burn it. But if you went after him, he and his tribe could always run away. This was one advantage of the Mongols that, in part, allowed them to build the largest empire the Earth had ever seen.

A Shogun

LYRICS

Flocabulary. Wanna learn
Something? Let me tell you what
Happened to me, man, Bully.

I woke up this morning in
Feudal Japan,
The guest of the shogun,
That dude was the man.
And even though the emperor
Ruled the land,
Sometimes the shogun
Bows down to no one,
That makes him the guy to know,
Elected by the daimyo.
They own the farmland,
Where the poor peasants try to
Grow crops and such,
But they're not too tough,
So the samurai defend them
When the block get rough.
Horses, swords and armor,
Bushido, code of honor,
Meant the samurai loves his lord
More than his mama.
And if there was drama,
They did something I'll never do,
To avoid shame or disgrace,
They commit seppuku.
That's suicide,
Maybe not for you and I,
But when you don't fear death,
It ain't much for you to die.
Many are Zen Buddhists,
They don't worry about their body,
Others are Shinto, they say
Everything is "kami."
I thanked the shogun, he said,

CONTEXT AND BACKGROUND

I woke up this morning in Feudal Japan...
For a long time, the Japanese looked to China for the structure of their government - they too set up a strong central government, and it was successful for a while. But eventually wealthy families began to ignore it and took control of their local areas, and a **feudal system** much like the one that grew up in Europe was established. Only it lasted longer than feudalism did anywhere else.

Though the emperor ruled the land, sometimes the shogun bows down to no one...
At the top of the social pyramid was the **emperor,** but he was largely a figurehead holding very little real power. The real power lay in the hands of the **shogun,** the supreme military leader. Being the highest-ranking person in the military was akin to being the ruler of the land. Many shogun had more power than even the emperor himself.

The shogun was chosen by powerful local lords, known as the **daimyo,** a word that means "great names." The daimyo owned large tracts of land and would rent it to peasants for farming; in the case of war, the daimyo would protect the peasants. But in order to maintain power and protect their land and peasants, the daimyo needed warriors. These were the samurai.

The samurai defend them when the block gets rough...
Samurai were knights much like the

93

knights of Europe. They wore armor, rode horses and were masters of the sword. They had their own code of honor called **Bushido,** which meant "the way of the warrior." This code placed great importance on bravery, loyalty and honor. Each samurai was loyal to his lord — and that loyalty was more important than his allegiance to the emperor or even to his family. As part of the Bushido, the samurai were expected to endure intense physical hardship and never complain, and they were expected to have no fear of death at all.

A Samurai

To avoid shame or disgrace, they commit seppuku...

If a samurai did something that displeased their lords, they might practice **seppuku,** a form of ceremonial suicide. Seppuku – also called hara-kiri or "belly splitting" – was a way to avoid shame and dishonor. Like the knights of Europe, samurai enjoyed very high status in society.

Many are Zen Buddhists, they don't worry about their body...

A particular type of Buddhism began to grow in popularity in Japan's Middle Ages. **Zen Buddhism** didn't emphasize prayer but self-control and meditation. It promoted the idea that the life of the body is not important. Many warriors picked up Zen Buddhism because it helped them rush into battle without fear.

Others are Shinto, they say everything is "kami"...

In the **Shinto** faith, a common Japanese religion in the Middle Ages, **"kami"** were divine spirits. But they weren't gods like gods in other polytheistic faiths; they were the spirits in all kinds of things, like natural forces and animals. They were guardian angels. And they were sometimes even considered to be in particularly gifted people.

"Come back anytime for karate...

At the same time in Japan, China, and some of the small islands in between, various forms of unarmed, physical combat developed. Unlike in the West, where hand-to-hand combat took the form of wrestling and boxing, martial arts in the East relied upon various moves, counters, kicks and grapples. **Karate** developed partly because the

LYRICS continued

"No prob." He got me.
"Come back anytime for
Karate and kamikazes,
Origami, plum sake in Nagasaki."
That's Flocabulary,
See Bully at the library.

Philippines and Thailand,
China, Taiwan, and Japan,
Indonesia and Malaysia,
That's Asia, man, that's Asia, man.

Korea and Mongolia,
Laos and Cambodia,
Vietnam and Bangladesh,
That's Asia, man, that's Asia, and...

The other day I tried to call up
My boy Tom,
You know Tom from MySpace?
But I guess the lines got crossed.
I ended up chatting with
Genghis Khan.
He told me what was going on
In Asia, man.
He spit a long rhyme for me;
He could flow for days,
About the Song Dynasty,
China's golden age.
Those were the days when they
Printed money to trade,
And the Song used gunpowder
In their bombs.
But Genghis Khan said that
It didn't last long,
'Cause he rode through with an
Army, many thousand strong,
Divided into groups of 10,
Khan would give the orders
And his men would start
Slaughtering the competition

daimyo around Okinawa in Japan tried to ban weapons in the 1400s and 1600s.

Kamikazes, Origami, plum sake in Nagasaki...

A mysterious and powerful wind (or typhoon) saved Japan from an invasion by the powerful Mongol armies. In 1274, 30,000 Mongol soldiers boarded hundreds of ships and sailed from what is now Korea toward Japan, poised to conquer it all. The Japanese had a much smaller navy, but thanks to a powerful wind that seemed to come from nowhere, the entire Mongol fleet was destroyed. Amazingly, almost the exact same thing happened seven years later: A typhoon destroyed another Mongol fleet. The Japanese called these typhoons **kamikaze**, or divine wind. This was the same name later given to Japanese fighter pilots in World War II who went on suicide missions. It's also the name of an alcoholic drink.

Sake, a type of wine made from rice, is a famous Japanese drink. Similar drinks were made 16,000 years ago in China. Back then, instead of using yeast to make the rice ferment into alcohol, people would chew on rice and then spit it into a bowl. They'd let that sit for a while; their saliva would slowly make the rice alcoholic. Then they'd drink it. Yum!

He told me what was going on in Asia, man...

In many ways, the people of Asia were far more advanced than the rest of the world during the Middle Ages. They had discovered gunpowder and were using it in their warfare. They had movable-type printing presses centuries before Europe did, and were making great developments in the sciences. Of course, this was also the time of marauding nomads like Genghis Khan, so it wasn't all good.

China is such a huge place that emperors had a hard time controlling it all. During the short-lived Sui Dynasty (581-618 BC), one emperor made an attempt to unify the north and south of the country. He had a canal built between China's two great rivers, the Yangtze and the Yellow. This was a massive undertaking – the man-made waterway, known as the **Grand Canal**, stretched more than 1,400 miles. It was all built by forced labor, but it was effective — communication and the transportation of troops was easier and faster than ever before, and trade flourished.

About the Song Dynasty, China's golden age...

The Song Dynasty (960-1279 AD) is remembered by the Chinese as a golden age, a time of great artistic and intellectual achievements that have shaped China all the way up to the present day. It was a time of busy cities, communication advances, economic growth and great artistic development. The government was run by officials who had to pass civil service exams (like they do today). Landscape paintings flourished, and architects played with new styles.

Those were the days when they printed money to trade...

The printing of literature grew by leaps and bounds during the Song Dynasty. People used printed monies to trade, and the Chinese began to use **gunpowder**-powered bombs in their warfare, which would revolutionize war across the globe. There were still setbacks during the Song Dynasty, however, it was known as a time of military weakness. The Chinese lost Tibet for the time being, and they were overrun by a new power emerging from the Gobi Desert — the Mongols.

But Genghis Khan said that it didn't last long...

Genghis Khan and his descendants built an empire unlike any the world had ever seen before. The **Mongol Empire** (1206-1405) spread from the Pacific Ocean to the Adriatic Sea. In square miles it was four times larger than the previous biggest empire — Alexander the Great's. this meant that more than 20 percent of the entire Earth was ruled by one man.

'Cause he rode through with an army, many thousand strong...

At the height of his powers, **Genghis Khan** (1162-1227) ruled over more territory than anyone ever had before. Originally named Temujin, he later took the title of Khan, which means "ruler." Khan was born around 1162 to a nomadic Mongol tribe. As he grew up, he began to build power for his people. Like other rulers, he did this through bloodshed.

First, he built a great army, the best the world knew at the time. Most of his army were horsemen: very fast, very organized and very good with the bow. Sources at the time describe the Mongol warriors as being able to hit a target 100 meters away while riding on horseback. That's longer than a football field! Part of the reason these troops were so accurate is that they made small, powerful bows that were far more advanced than anything the Europeans were using. Also, because of specially designed saddles and

LYRICS continued

When he told them to.
With bows and horses,
Those the boldest troops
The world had ever seen.
Khan knew many women,
Biblically.
Rewards for the best;
That's a meritocracy,
And Khan had a fifth of the world
At his knees.

Hook

stirrups, archers on horseback could turn backwards and fire arrows even as they retreated.

Divided into groups of 10...
Genghis Khan organized the Mongol soldiers into groups based on the decimal system. Units were built from groups of 10 (Arbat), 100 (Zuut), 1,000 (Myangat), and 10,000 (Tumen), each with a leader reporting to the next higher level. Two to five Tumens would then form a *hordu*, or field army. In Europe, people called the Mongols the "barbarian hordes;" the word *horde* comes from "hordu."

Mongolian Horse-Archers

With bows and horses, those the boldest troops the world had ever seen...

Khan used his troops to unite all of Mongolia's tribes. He then moved to take the lands around him, starting in 1207 with attacks on Xi-Xia, which is now China and part of Tibet. The warlord kept on after that, pushing both east and west. He was brutally efficient. Most estimates put the number of casualties left in his wake in the millions. For this reason, he is a very controversial figure in history. Should we celebrate the accomplishments of someone who killed so much? Or is Ghengis Khan just like Alexander the Great or Julius Caesar, who used victories in war to build vast empires?

War is always a gruesome, terrible event. Throughout history in most cultures, war has meant killing, pillaging (stealing), destruction, rape and often taking captives as slaves. It's easy to read a sentence like "Alexander the Great conquered Egypt" without realizing that conquering meant bloodshed, families torn apart and innocent people killed for no reason.

Khan knew many women, biblically...

A recent study found that a huge number (8 percent) of men who live near Mongolia today have nearly identical Y chromosomes. Some scientists believe that this is because they are all descendents of Genghis Khan, who reportedly fathered many, many children. If this is true, it means that 16 million people on Earth today are relatives of Genghis Khan.

Rewards for the best, that's a meritocracy...

One good thing about Khan's ruling style is that leadership positions were fairly open to people of different races, cultures and faiths. Khan set up something like a **meritocracy**, a system based on merit. In this type of system, it doesn't necessarily matter if you are the grandson of a prince; what matters is how smart and strong you are.

And Khan had a fifth of the world at his knees...

At the time of Genghis Khan's death in 1227, the Mongol Empire extended from the Pacific Ocean across Asia to the Caspian Sea. Even after his death, the empire continued to expand until 1279, when it covered an amazing 22% of the Earth's total land area.

Among Genghis's successors was **Kublai Khan**, his grandson. Unlike other Khans that preceded him, though, Kublai Khan ruled out of China. He lived in Beijing, where he set up the Yuan Dynasty, the first non-Chinese dynasty to rule China. He was in command in China when the Italian explorer **Marco Polo** paid his famous visit to the East. By most accounts Kublai was not as nasty as his grandfather and tried to use diplomacy when possible. When it wasn't, however, he was happy to attack.

HISTORY SPEAKS

"Do not follow the ideas of others, but learn to listen to the
voice within yourself. Your body and mind will become
clear and you will realize the unity of all things."

– Dogen Zenji, Zen Buddhist Teacher, 1200-1253

Imagine if your mom or dad said this to you:

"With heaven's aid I have conquered for you a huge
empire. But my life was too short to achieve the conquest
of the world. That task is left for you."

– Genghis Khan (talking to his son)

INTRO

Europeans and Asians weren't the only ones spilling blood for land and power. Africa too was home to various groups bumping into one another, struggling for the upper hand. Africa was, and is, an extremely diverse land. The vast majority of Africans lived in small communities and did what small town people do: work the land for food. They told stories, raised their young as best they could, celebrated their holidays, and mourned when their loved ones were lost to war or famine. But various empires also emerged, boosted by trade routes and bountiful natural resources. The mighty empires of Ghana and Mali are the most famous.

A Mosque in Timbuktu

LYRICS

Man,
I noticed when we study history,
We spend a lot of time
Studying light-skinned people.
It's not quite equal;
Why don't we study Africans
As much as we study Europeans?
Well, there's two reasons:
One, they had an oral tradition,
Like spitting rap lyrics
With no writtens.
Sitting in a semi circle,
Listening to a wise man's wisdom,
There's no books in those traditions.
Reason two: racism, cultural elitism,
White people
Controlled the system;
Blacks and Asians didn't.
So some white people like,
"I don't care if you speak,
Swahili, Zulu, or Arabic, kid.
I'm not hearing it."
But listen to the richness
Of these traditions,
In Africa,
The griot telling tales in town.
In Africa,
Growing coffee by the pound.
In Africa,
Languages - there's 2,000.

*Kenya, Zimbabwe,
Botswana and Mali,
Uganda and Ghana,
That's Africa, that's Africa.*

*That's Africa, Somalia,
Mozambique, and Zambia,*

CONTEXT AND BACKGROUND

We spend a lot time studying light-skinned people...
It was common, not very long ago, to learn "world history" by spending 90% of your time reading about Europe and 10% learning about the rest of the world. Nearly everyone now agrees that this approach to history was **Eurocentric** (centered on Europe).

Reason two: racism, cultural elitism...
It used to be that Europe was called Western civilization, Asia was Eastern civlization, and Africa and the Americas were considered "uncivilized." We now know that this view is extremely flawed and is rooted in ignorance, racism and feelings of cultural superiority. Recently, there has been a push to teach more about African, American and Asian civilizations. But history books always leave things out. What do you think: Is the way we teach history fair?

In Africa, the griot telling tales in town...
A **griot** is a West African poet, praise singer, and wandering musician who was full of ancient and contemporary knowledge and would move from town to town telling stories and singing songs. Some of these songs passed down ancient fables and histories; others were meant to get laughs. A griot might gossip or poke fun at people, too. Some scholars have noted that griots also had to freestyle by commenting on things that he saw as he was singing.

101

FLOCAB SPITS FACTS LIKE AN ALMANAC

The rapper Nas has used African history in his lyrics as a way of spreading knowledge and encouraging kids to dream big. In his song "I Can," he raps about "Timbuktu, where every race came to get books." He also raps about the invasions into Africa and colonization: "Africa was almost robbed naked." Unfortunately, later African history provides a lot of proof for this claim.

In Africa, growing coffee by the pound...

Coffee was first discovered in Ethiopia around 900. It was exported into the Arab world, where it gradually became popular because of its ability to keep people awake. It is now one of the most widely drunk beverages in the world, and Ethiopia remains a top producer.

In Africa, languages - there's 2,000...

An estimated **2,000 languages** are spoken in Africa to this day. One hundred of them are considered "major languages" in that they are spoken by hundreds of thousands or millions of people. The huge linguistic diversity of many African countries has made language policy an extremely important issue. The policies being developed nowadays are mostly aimed at multilingualism, because when languages die, so do stories, traditions and histories.

Rich with the camels and gold were kings of Ghana...

The modern state of Ghana is located about 500 miles from the Middle Ages' **Kingdom of Ghana** (750-1076). The Niger River flowed between the Sahara Desert to the north and the tropical forest along the coast. Ghana was a largely rural place, ruled by kings who had absolute power. These kings were themselves called "Ghana," a name that means "warrior king." They amassed great wealth due to two things — **camels and gold**. There was a lot of gold to be mined in West Africa, and the introduction of the camel allowed goods to be hauled much farther than ever before, thus greatly expanding trade.

They used their gold for trade, they had it made...

West African gold was traded for a variety of goods; it made Ghanaian

Mansa Musa

LYRICS continued

Congo and Swaziland,
That's Africa, man.

From the rivers of Niger to the
Deserts of Sahara,
Rich with the camels and gold
Were kings of Ghana.
They used their gold for trade,
They had it made,
An oasis in the shade in the days
When roads weren't paved.
So, call the Berbers up, nomadic,
They could further us
To cultures, religions and folks
Who never heard of us.
Oh, now they're murderers
'Cause fighting's erupted?
The kingdom of Ghana
Wiped out by 1200?
After that came Sundiata Keita,
A great Mali leader,
"Lion King," known to the people.
He grew the lands until Mansa
Musa came along,
Who was really strong,
The most famous king of them all.
Trekking Sahara with over
60,000 followers,
The capital of Timbuktu,
Where lived astronomers.
The promise of a new world
Had come true
Through manuscripts of Timbuktu,
A true story.

kings very wealthy. Often, they
exchanged gold for salt, which they
used to preserve food. For a long time
the two commodities were worth
roughly the same amount of money.
The people of Ghana were also expert
iron makers and used the country's iron
ore reserves to make weapons.

So call the Berbers up, nomadic, they
could further us…
The Ghanaians didn't usually deliver
their merchandise themselves, but
left it to the **Berbers**. The Berbers
were a nomadic people who used
camels and carved out trade routes
across the Sahara, traveling in great
caravans. They would take goods from
Ghana — and items the Ghanaians
had acquired from the people who
lived south of them — and resell
them in Egypt and at ports along the
Mediterranean Sea.

Oh, now they're murderers 'cause
fighting's erupted…
When Arab Muslims moved through
North Africa in the seventh century,
they converted many of the nomadic
Berber people to their faith. Some of
the Berbers eventually formed their
own Muslim empire in northwest Africa
and parts of Spain, an empire that
eventually conquered the empire of
Ghana.

The kingdom of Ghana wiped out by
1200…
By 1200, the Kingdom of Ghana had
completely fallen apart. The empire
had fought wars with Berber tribes
and eventually with the Mali leader
Sundiata Keita. Plus, Ghanaians
suffered from food shortages due
to reduced trade and the ever-
expanding Sahara desert, which

each year covered more and more farmland with sand (the Sahara is still growing today).

After that came Sundiata Keita, a great Mali leader...

Sundiata (the "Lion King") took over the Ghanaian capital in 1240 and began a new era of West African dominance. This time it was the **Kingdom of Mali**. Centered on the hub city of Timbuktu, Mali got its wealth from trading in gold, and from the Niger River Valley, which gave this savanna country, where large grasslands stretched for miles, fertile soil for growing crops. By 1235 Mali had built a mighty kingdom that spread from the savanna country to the edge of the Sahara desert to the Atlantic Ocean.

He grew the lands until Mansa Musa came along...

Mansa Musa was the most famous king of the Mali empire. He was a pragmatic ruler, dividing his empire into provinces. Trusted governors ruled each province, and cities and towns had mayors.

Trekking Sahara with over 60,000 followers...

Like many of the other leaders of Mali, Mansa Musa was a Muslim, and he made a legendary trek across the Sahara in a huge caravan in 1324. More than 60,000 people went with him, along with 100 camels, each carrying 300 pounds of gold. He was on his way to Mecca and Medina, the most holy sites for Muslims. When he returned, Musa brought Muslim books with him and spread the faith. And he built fancy mosques like he'd seen in his travels.

The capital of Timbuktu, where lived astronomers...

Timbuktu was the capital during Mansa Musa's reign. It was a booming hub, a center of commerce, art and learning. The city sat at something of a crossroads. To the north was the Sahara desert and its great camel

caravans. Beyond the desert sands was the Arab world. To the south was what is called sub-Saharan Africa. The city had an air of mystique about it — perhaps because of all the gold that traveled through. Timbuktu grew into an important center of Islam and academia. A treasure trove of documents called the **Timbuktu Manuscripts** has proven to modern scholars that the city was ahead of its time in the study of astronomy, mathematics, medicine and chemistry.

Desert Caravan

CHAPTER 15:

AFRICAN PROVERBS

INTERLUDE

A Griot

INTRO

Most African history, stories and knowledge weren't passed down through books, but via family members, singers and storytellers. Virtually all of Africa's many cultures have a rich tradition of proverbs – little sayings that contain big wisdom. The proverbs from this chapter are just a few of the thousands and thousands of proverbs from Africa's history. See if you can figure out what each one means before you read the description.

AFRICAN PROVERBS

LYRICS

Mother Africa, I know that your
People pass knowledge through
Stories and sayings and rhymes. I
Know your people are very wise.
What do the people of Libya say?

The people of Libya say:
*The camel does not see the bend
In its neck.*

What do the Fula people say?

The Fula people say:
Patience can cook a stone.

What do the Ashanti say?

The Ashanti say:
*If you understand the beginning
Well, the end will not trouble you.*

What do the people of Tanzania
Say?

The people of Tanzania say:
Sticks in a bundle are unbreakable.

What do the Ethiopians say?

The Ethiopians say:
*When one is in love, a cliff
Becomes a meadow.*

And what do the Ewe people say?

The Ewe people say:
*Until the lion has his or her own
Storyteller, the hunter will always
Have the best part of the story.*

CONTEXT AND BACKGROUND

The people of Libya say: The camel does not see the bend in its neck...
Meaning: It is easy to see the faults in other people, but harder to see your own.

For hundreds of years, the camel was the car of the desert, and in many places it still is. Able to travel long stretches without water, it was the perfect animal for transporting people, food and goods across the seemingly endless sands of the Sahara. In Libya, the camels have long necks that are curved sharply. Locals, who think the camel's neck is unattractive, believe that a camel cannot see its own "ugliness."

The Fula people say: Patience can cook a stone...
Meaning: Patience can solve any problem, no matter how impossible it seems.

The Fula (or Fulbe) people live in many countries in West and Central Africa. Many Fula groups are nomadic, herding cattle and sheep across the African plains. The Fula people eat all kinds of food, but they don't eat stones. This proverb takes something that seems impossible (cooking a stone) and says it can be achieved with patience.

The Ashanti say: If you understand the beginning well, the end will not trouble you...
Meaning: Knowledge will free you from worry.

The Ashanti people are a major ethnic group who live in central

107

Ghana. They have a long, rich history that includes the Ashanti Kingdom, which ruled the land around present-day Ghana in the 17th century. The Ashanti are a very proud people who believe that they have been chosen by God to do good in the world. They place a strong value on doing things well and not rushing or being lazy, and they value knowledge. Stories from ancestors are passed down every evening after dinner.

The people of Tanzania say: Sticks in a bundle are unbreakable...

Meaning: Even if people have little power on their own, sticking together makes them very strong.

Tanzania is a country on the east coast of Africa, bordering the Indian Ocean. The people there are a mix of original Bantu speakers and Arab traders who built settlements in the first century. They speak Swahili, but come from many different ethnic groups. But despite their varying cultures, the people know that sticking together makes them stronger.

The Ethiopians say: When one is in love, a cliff becomes a meadow...

Meaning: Love makes the whole world seem wonderful (but also makes you a little crazy).

Ethiopia is one of the oldest countries in the world. Fossilized bones from some of the earliest human ancestors have been found there, and powerful civilizations have called Ethiopia home since around 1000 BC. The famous Greek historian Herodotus once remarked that he thought the Ethiopians were the tallest and most beautiful people in the world. They were fierce fighters; they created powerful empires and successfully repelled all European invasions until the 20th century. But Ethiopians were also peace-loving people with a strong appreciation for stories and art.

Many African proverbs mention love as a powerful force that can make rational people do irrational things. Love was celebrated in Africa, but people who were in love were sometimes made fun of.

The Ewe people say: Until the lion has his or her own storyteller, the hunter will always have the best part of the story...

Meaning: You can never really understand something unless you get both sides of the story. And history is written by the conquerors.

The Ewe are one of the major ethnic groups in Benin, Ghana, and Togo. They mostly form farming communities, but also hunt and fish. Hunters are revered in the communities that rely on hunted prey for food, so a hunter who returns with a lion or steer will have an audience who wants to hear all about the kill. People listen to the story, but they also realize that the hunter might be exaggerating to make himself look better. They're only getting one side of the story – the lion, after all, is dead.

HISTORY SPEAKS

"When the missionaries came to Africa they had the Bible and we had the land. They said, 'Let us pray.' We closed our eyes. When we opened them we had the Bible and they had the land."

- Bishop Desmond Tutu

CHAPTER 16:
THE EMPIRES OF ISLAM

570 to 1923

INTRO

While the powers of Europe were moving through the Middle Ages, in parts of Asia, Africa and the Middle East, various Islamic peoples were building their own impressive societies. There were the Turks, whose massive Ottoman Empire rose to power in 1299; the Mughals, who ruled India; and the Safavids, who brought greatness back to the Persian peoples. These groups all shared the Muslim faith and, taken together, comprise the Muslim empires (or empires of Islam).

These new imperial powers were marked by a close relationship between government and religion. They prospered throughout the Middle Ages, but by the end of the 19th century, all three had declined significantly. By the early 20th century, with the Ottomans' defeat in World War I, the last Muslim empire collapsed.

The Taj Mahal

LYRICS

Mecca, Medina, Arabia, uh huh,
We bow down and we raise it up,
Uh huh,
Imams guide Islam,
So get to your mosque,
And read your Qur'an.

Now deep in the desert,
This guy called Muhammad,
Heard a voice calling, he's like,
"Yo, I'm on it."
Started in Mecca,
And he conquered it,
Then it spread out
Across the continent.
Converting Bedouin tribes
With some threats and knives,
Plus some smart tactics and
Tolerance in their lives.
"Mecca," boy,
Yeah that's where I come from,
By 632 Arabia was Muslim.
Muhammad regarded
Christians and Jews
As people of the book; said,
"Just let 'em do what they do."
But he spoke of jihad,
That's a struggle for faith,
Said if you die for Islam,
You get the blessings of God.
His successors disagreed and
Fought like Tupac,
You're either caliph or you're not.
Sunnis follow the way,
But it's disputed,
Shia's only 10 percent,
So they're persecuted.
Muslim empire expanded

CONTEXT AND BACKGROUND

This guy called Muhammad heard a voice...
When **Muhammad** heard the voice of God, or Allah in Arabic, speaking to him, he started telling people about it. This was the year 610, in his hometown, **Mecca** (in present day Saudi Arabia). Mecca's rulers didn't like what he was saying, so they kicked him out. Muhammad moved to **Medina**, and he and his followers began spreading their faith to nomadic tribes, ambushing caravans from Mecca. Finally, he rode back into Mecca and faced little resistance. He'd become a religious prophet and political leader.

Converting the Bedouin tribes with some threats and knives, plus some smart tactics...
Islam spread very quickly under the leadership of Muhammad. He combined military conquest with strategies that made it desirable in society to join the faith.

By 632 Arabia was Muslim...
The term **Arabia** comes from the Persian word *Arabaya*. It was the name given to the land to the west and south of Mesopotamia, which basically meant the land between the Persian Gulf, the Red Sea, and the Mediterranean. By Muhammad's death in 632, most of the Arabian Peninsula was Muslim.

Muhammad regarded Christians and Jews, as people of the book...
Despite all of the hatred, misunderstanding and ignorance that exists today between Jews, Christians

111

and Muslims, all three groups are closely related. Jesus and Moses are both prophets in the Qur'an.

But he spoke of jihad, that's a struggle for faith...

Jihad is an important principle in the Qur'an. It means "a struggle to defend Islam." Many Muslims interpret the word to mean a war to defend their faith. Others believe that jihad can be

an internal struggle. But Muhammad promised that those who died fighting for Islam would be rewarded in heaven.

You're either caliph or you're not...

The separation of church and state was not an important principle to Muslims: Their religious leaders were (and often still are) their political leaders as well. This dates all the way back to the founding of the Islamic faith under Mohammed. He was both the spiritual and political leader of the Muslims. When he died, the next leader was called a **caliph**, which means successor or representative. These men were considered both the head of government and the head of the Islamic faith.

One of the most famous caliphs was **Harun al-Rashid** (763-809 AD) a great ruler of Baghdad. He was the head of the east when Charlemagne was ruling the west. The two admired each other. Rashid's reign was characterized by a great deal of artistic and intellectual growth. He surrounded himself with some of the most brilliant minds of his day. Some say he is the hero in many of the stories in the *Arabian Nights*.

Sunnis follow the way, but it's disputed...

If you read the news, you know that even today there is a lot of tension between two groups of Muslims: the **Sunni** and the **Shia** or Shiites. The split between Sunni and Shia Muslims goes back to 661, when the fourth caliph after Muhammad, a man named Ali, was killed. A big disagreement ensued about who should be the next caliph. Sunnis believed that the first four caliphs, or heirs to Muhammed, were

LYRICS continued

In Pakistan,
And through North Africa
Into Spain.
Turkish Ottomans came in
And they took over,
Now the sultan's commanding
Some slave soldiers.
Others moved on India,
Bringing Urdu,
Fight with spears;
Spears hurt more than words do.
"Babur the Tiger" earned his stripes,
Fighting for the Mughals,
Staying out the trouble.

Hook

My navigator wasn't made
By Lincoln,
My navigator was me,
My own intuition.
Used the sun, moon, and stars,
The astrolabe,
A director with good sense
Like an old-school GPS.
Bow in grace, five times I pray,
'Cause in Allah is where
I place my faith.
Speaking Swahili
Brought to you by Africans,
Because they built mosques
On their continent.
The numbers you use,
We brought them to you,
Arabic numerals from Hindus
In 1202.
Cleanliness, yeah,
That's next to godliness,
And who but Allah is the purest?
Our doctors knew how
Blood moved,

the rightful successors to the prophet. Their descendants ruled the Arab world until after World War I. The word *Sunni* means the way of the prophet.

Shia's only 10 percent, so they're persecuted...

The Shia were (and still are) a smaller group. They thought that only one of those first four caliphs was legitimate – the one named Ali – and only his heirs should rule. It might seem like a small difference, but it meant that these people were telling their rulers, "You don't have the right to rule us." This made those rulers (and other Sunnis) upset.

Muslim empire expanded in Pakistan...

The **Seljuks** came out of Turkmenistan in about 950. They were nomads who decided to settle down in what was then Persia (now Iran). Before long they conquered what is now Iraq, and by 1070 they had moved to take what is today Syria and parts of the Byzantine Empire. For the better part of a couple of centuries, the Seljuks were a major power in the Middle East. They fought challenges from the Mongols and other peoples before finally falling in 1192.

And through North Africa into Spain...

The Islamic empires also spread through North Africa from Arabs to Berbers, who then conquered Spain. Called **Moors** by Europeans, the Muslims in Spain ruled a strong state that, some say, far exceeded the rest of Europe when it came to education, technological advances and philosophies. Christians and Jews were free to practice their respective religions, as long as they paid a special tax.

FLOCAB SPITS FACTS LIKE AN ALMANAC

Just as there are Christian, Jewish, Buddhist and Atheistic rappers, a whole slew of Muslim rappers have recently appeared. Many of them are Muslim-Americans whose goal it is to spread knowledge about Muslims in an age where stupidity and ignorance often win. One group, Native Deen, even has a song about three Muslim prophets: Moses, Jesus and Muhammad. On Muhammad's life, they rap: "He could teach about Allah without his people getting beaten / His folks back in Mecca couldn't stand all the preachings."

Turkish Ottomans came in, and they took over...

Out of the ashes of the Seljuk kingdom rose the **Ottoman Empire**. One of the last Seljuk kings, Osman, founded the new power. In about 1299 he began expanding from the region of what is now Turkey toward Europe. For several centuries the Ottomans fought European peoples. The Mongols put pressure on them to the east, so they tried to acquire new territory in the west, which was European. They conquered Greece in 1352, and in 1453 they delivered a huge blow by taking the seat of the Byzantine Empire, Constantinople. By 1517 they assumed control of Egypt, as well. Ottoman sultans remained a forceful presence on the edge of Europe all the way up to the 1920s.

Now the sultan's commanding some slave soldiers...

The Ottomans' elite military forces were called **janissaries**. They were Christians and other non-Muslims who had been taken as captives of war or from their families at a very young age. They were slaves in that they were involuntarily taken, but they were paid a monthly salary.

Others moved on India, bringing Urdu...

Muslim Turks also moved toward India, fighting fiercely with civilizations there. By the early 1200s they had finally conquered northern India. The Muslims set up a new empire in India called the **Delhi Sultanate**, while the Turks and Arabs spread the Urdu language throughout the region's north.

LYRICS continued

Health is vital,
So we built medical schools.
Attached them to temples
To show our gratitude,
Caring about people,
I live amongst you.
As a Muslim, if you get the chance,
Head on down to Mecca
For the experience.
Like Muhammad Battuta
And his journeys through
Egypt, China, Sumatra
And Timbuktu.

Hook

"Babur the Tiger" earned his stripes...

The **Mughal Empire** was a product of various Central Asian invasions into the Indian subcontinent. It was founded by prince Babur ("the Tiger") in 1526 with the destruction of the Delhi Sultanate. Though Babur would die soon after founding his new empire, it would thrive under later leaders.

Fighting for the Mughals, staying out the trouble...

One of those later leaders was **Akbar the Great**, who achieved fame simply by being nice – or rather, tolerant. Living in a place where people held all sorts of different beliefs, from Buddhism to Hinduism to Islam, he recognized the importance of simply getting along. Though he was raised Muslim, he was intrigued by other religions and ways of life. Besides being open-minded, Akbar was a fine military strategist. He created the largest empire India had seen in almost 2,000 years. How? Largely by the use of gunpowder. This was 1600, and he used heavy artillery on old stone fortresses. It was very effective.

So get to your mosque...

Mosques are the holy houses of Islam – places of worship like a Christian church or Jewish temple. As such, they can be found throughout the world wherever Muslim people gathered. Historians can trace the spread of Islam by looking at places where there are mosques and dating them. One very famous mosque is the **Dome of the Rock** in Jerusalem. Muslims believe that it was the place where Muhammed ascended into Paradise. The most distinctive features of mosques are their domes and **minarets**, the tall towers from which

115

religious officials call the faithful to prayer.

Used the sun, moon, and stars, the astrolabe...

Because Muslims were required to pray toward Mecca, they had to have a good sense of direction – or, better yet, a tool that would help them orient themselves in the world. Early Muslims borrowed the Greek **astrolabe**, a device used to determine the position of celestial objects like the sun. Muslim scientists improved on the Greek designs and used the astrolabe to develop a calendar, figure out prayer times and orient mosques and people toward Mecca. This simple device would later change the world, because it allowed sailors to navigate by the stars – which led to the great age of exploration.

Speaking Swahili brought to you by Africans...

Because Islam spread over the continent, there are many mosques in Africa. Another result is **Swahili**, which is both a language and a culture, stemming from the meeting of Arab and African peoples. The language itself is based in African Bantu, but it incorporates a lot of Arabic terms, probably because the Swahili people were Muslims and read the Qur'an. The Swahili language and culture developed in eastern Africa, and is today the national language of several African nations.

Arabic numerals from Hindus in 1202...

The numbers we know and use today in counting and mathematics come from the work of Arab scholars. They took the numbers that were used by Hindus in India and made them their own. By 1202 an Italian mathematician named Fibonacci brought them to Europe, and they gradually evolved into our present-day number system.

Our doctors knew how blood moved...

The Arabs made some major developments in medicine. Common and accepted practices today, from the importance of cleanliness and hygiene to the use of cauterization (when a doctor burns you to heal you), date back to old Arabic times. Arab physicians discovered many medicines we still use today, and they were the first to understand essential workings of the body, like the circulatory system. Hospitals in Baghdad and Cairo were models of their day during the Middle Ages. Medical schools were often attached to Egyptian temples.

Like Muhammad Battuta and his journeys...

Muhammad ibn Battuta (c. 1304-1368) was a great traveler from what is now Tangier in Morocco. Like most Muslims, he made the pilgrimage to Mecca. But unlike everybody else, he developed wanderlust while doing so – he couldn't stop traveling. He went to Egypt, Syria, the Maldives, Timbuktu, and other parts of Africa, Sumatra, and China. He became famous for writing about his journeys, and his works helped historians get a glimpse of many of these places that they wouldn't otherwise have gotten.

A Muslim Palace Guard

CHAPTER 17:

HAY NATIVOS

Mesoamerican Civilizations: 1800 BC to 1500 AD

A lonesome warrior stands in fear of what the future brings,
He will never hear the beating drums or the songs his brothers sing.
Our many nations once stood tall and ranged from shore to shore
But most are gone and few remain and the buffalo roam no more.
– Tommy Flamewalker Manasco

Looking at America today, it is easy to see the social, cultural, and architectural heritage of the white settlers, but it is much harder to find the heritage of the millions of original Americans who populated North and South America. Mostly, this is because huge numbers of those Native Americans were conquered and killed, either by new diseases or European guns. Cultural ignorance and a self-centered worldview allowed the white settlers to dismiss the Native Americans as "savages."

We now know a lot more about the civilizations that lived in America before the land got that name. We know about the many tribes and societies that existed off the rich soil or followed the great herds of buffalo. We know about the three major empires of America – the Maya, Aztec and Inca civilizations. These people built large cities to live in and giant temples to worship their gods. They didn't live in paradise – owning slaves was common in Mesoamerica. But they also demonstrated lots of practical knowledge – from astronomy to farming techniques to medicines. These were the original Americans.

LYRICS

Hey boys and girls, today we're going to be talking about Mesoamerica. After the Ice Age, people began moving across the Bering Strait into North America. They left northeast Asia and migrated through what is now Alaska, all the way down to South America. By the Middle Ages, these people had gotten organized. Some of these civilizations were far more advanced than the Europeans would ever imagine.

In modern-day Veracruz,
Archaeologists
Pick up a pair of clues.
They saw pyramids
And giant stone heads,
And learned they belonged
To the Olmecs.
They discovered
The mother culture,
The first cities, artisans, sculptors.
Now that's around 1200 BC,
The Maya came next
With similarities.
Advanced agriculturists
In the Yucatan,
With city-states,
The illest that you could plan.
Like Tikal, they found in Guatemala,
They used intercropping and
Reservoirs for water.
They had a calendar
And a writing system,
But a ball game

CONTEXT AND BACKGROUND

Sometime around 1000 BC, huge earth mounds began to appear in various parts of North America. These were grass-covered structures made of dirt, shaped in a variety of ways – cones, ridges and pyramids. Historians believe they were ceremonial and funeral mounds, and they called the people who built them **moundbuilders**. By about 700 AD most of these peoples had begun to farm, rather than roam as nomads.

The **Puebloans** lived in what is now southwestern United States in the first century AD. They were famous for their ceramics and beautiful wall paintings. But what was perhaps most remarkable about them was the way they built their homes — they carved them right out of the cliffs. People still visit these structures today at places like Mesa Verde National Park in Colorado. Historians remain unsure why the Puebloans abandoned these wall-side villages around 1300.

Archaeologists pick up a pair of clues. **The Olmec civilization** was a lost, forgotten civilization until 1862. That year, a man named José Melgar y Serrano was wandering around the forest when he stumbled upon a giant head made of stone. Later, many more giant heads were found, as well as some pyramids – the remnants of the Olmec civilization.

Learned they belonged to the Olmecs. They discovered the mother culture... The first culture to build cities in the Americas was probably the Olmecs. They lived along the Gulf of Mexico

119

FLOCAB SPITS FACTS LIKE AN ALMANAC

Don't have horses, so they run the fastest...

You may have an image in your head of Native Americans riding around on horses. In fact, Native Americans had never seen horses until the Spanish brought them over from Europe. You may also think that Italians have been making pizza for thousands of years. But, no. They didn't have any tomatoes. Just as horses were native to Europe and Asia, tomatoes were native to the Americas. Once the Spanish brought tomatoes back to Europe, though, the Italians began to use it as the basis for lots of their food.

beginning around 1200 BC and built great pyramids in the jungle. The Olmec culture is sometimes called the mother culture of Mesoamerica because they strongly influenced the societies that would follow.

The first cities, artisans, sculptors...

Some of the Olmecs were sculptors and artisans, and some historians believe they created the first writing system in the Americas. They were a ritualistic people, governed by both kings and priests, and they were fascinated with the jaguar, something that many other Mesoamerican cultures would pick up on. They considered this jungle cat a manifestation of God on Earth. They also traded with other peoples, and may even have come up with a calendar. Olmec items have been found in various parts of Central America, but they're most famous for the large **stone heads** they carved. Imagine having to sculpt a rock the size of a car into the likeness of a person without metal tools! Historians don't know as much about them as some other ancient societies.

The Maya came next with similarities...

The next great civilization in the Americas was probably the **Maya**. In fact, archaeologists considered them the first for a long time. They were a farming people who lived on the Yucatan Peninsula between 300 and 900 AD. The Maya bore a lot of similarities to the Olmec.

Advanced agriculturists in the Yucatan...

Most Mayan men lived in villages, and were advanced agriculturalists. We know this because they practiced

LYRICS continued

Where you could die a victim.
Slavery, sacrifice, it was a risky time,
And we don't know why they
Disappeared in 869!

Sudamerica, Centroamerica,
Mesoamerica:
Hay nativos! (There are natives!)
Olmec, Maya, Aztec, Inca,
The original American thinkers.

Sudamerica, Centroamerica,
Mesoamerica:
Hay nativos! (There are natives!)
Tikal, Tenochtitlan,
Machu Picchu: cities of some of
The original people.

Who has next?
Oh, that would be the Aztecs,
Don't have horses,
So they run the fastest.
They kept control of a portion of
The atlas in Mexico,
Around Lake Texcoco.
They're like, "If we roam we might
Not be strong,"
So they built a big city,
Tenochtitlan.
A city on a lake;
They bathed twice a day,
Plant corn, grind it up,
Make it into pancakes.
They had schools
Every kid attended,
They learned how to write,
Yep, also how to fight.
Imagine if one day
Your teacher was like,
"After math, I'll show you
How to attack with an ax."

intercropping, where certain crops
are planted together, using one to
stimulate the growth of the other.

*With city-states, the illest that you
could plan. Like Tikal, they found in
Guatemala...*
But they also built huge cities. Some
archaeologists estimate that one
such municipality, **Tikal**, now found in
Guatemala, was home to as many as
100,000 residents at one time. There
were more than 3,000 buildings there,
some towering high over the jungle.
The Mayans were very advanced
in mathematics, astronomy and
engineering. In Tikal this manifested in
their construction of reservoirs to hold
water for the city. The water moved
between manmade lakes using
gravity in such a manner that they
must have had a deep knowledge of
mathematics.

*They had a calendar and a writing
system...*
Like the Olmecs, the Maya also
constructed pyramids, were great
artists, created a writing system, and
definitely had a calendar (and an
accurate one at that). They built
actual city-states across Central
America complete with temples,
palaces and small stadiums.

*But a ball game where you could be a
victim. Slavery, sacrifice, it was a risky
time...*
For all of their artistic and scientific
sophistication, though, they were a
brutal people. They had slaves, and
human sacrifice was common. They
played a rubber ball game that usually
ended in the losers being ritually
killed. And they were fierce warriors.
Historians don't know why their culture

largely disappeared in 869 AD.

Who has next? Oh, that would be the Aztecs...

When the Spanish conquistadors smashed their way into the Americas in the 16th century, they were amazed by the **Aztecs**. They were a very sophisticated people. Like the Maya they had a calendar and a writing system, and were religious and warlike.

They built a big city, Tenochtitlan...

Sometime between 1200 and 1325, the Aztec people transformed from nomadic hunters to farmers. The story goes that the Aztec leader at the time was told by their god, Huitzilopochtli, to go to an island in **Lake Texcoco** and set up their homeland. So that's what they did.

They built a large city, **Tenochtitlan**, right on an island in the middle of the lake. They built bridges, or causeways, that connected the island to the mainland. The Aztecs were very clever about using the water all around for *chinampa*, which were small, man-made floating gardens. Historians estimate the population in Tenochtitlan to have been about 200,000 at its height. It's where Montezuma, the famous leader of the Aztecs when the Spanish invaded, had his palace. His gilded home and the rest of the city were destroyed in 1521 by the Spanish conquistador Hernandez Cortes. But archaeologists

Machu Picchu

LYRICS continued

Aztecs would take slaves
And captives from their enemies;
That's just part of their tactics.
The fact is,
They were sharper than a cactus,
They sacrificed humans,
It seemed like madness.

Hook

While the Aztecs were in Mexico,
The Incas were building a kingdom,
Exceptional.
At its height in the 12th century,
It stretched from Ecuador to Chile.
Essentially based at Peru,
In the city of Cuzco,
To connect various tribes
They used roads.
They built aqueducts in the Andes,
And they farmed terraces,
Y'all, to feed families.
We're talking
Over a million residents,
They were developing
Some of the best medicines.
Plus, the king had style,
Machu Picchu –
The city of the clouds.
But from the ground,
It vanished, the secret,
Never found by the Spanish.
The people asked
Was it used for astronomy?
9,000 feet,
And the views are astonishing.

Hook

have learned a lot about Aztec culture from the ruins of Tenochtitlan, where modern-day Mexico City stands.

They bathed twice a day, plant corn, grind it up, make it into pancakes...
The most common Aztec foods were corn, beans, squash, chilies and tomatoes, all important staples of the Mexican diet to this day. Although they were largely vegetarian, the Aztec people also ate insects like grasshoppers and ants, which are full of protein.

They had schools that every kid attended, they learned how to write, yep, also how to fight...
Through age 14, a child's education was in the hands of his or her parents. Then at 15, every boy and girl was sent to school, though they were taught different things: Girls learned about taking care of the house and raising children, while boys were taught how to read, write and fight.

Aztecs would take slaves and captives from their enemies...
Aztecs seemed to believe that the gods (there were more than 1,000 of them) had sacrificed themselves to create the Earth. So it made sense to the Aztecs that they would have to **sacrifice humans** in order to honor and serve the gods. The Aztecs didn't want to sacrifice the people who lived in their own cities and villages, so they relied on taking slaves and captives from other villages and tribes.

They sacrificed humans, it seems like madness...
The Aztecs took human sacrifice to an amazing level. By their own accounts, they once sacrificed thousands of

people in just a few days while they rebuilt a large pyramid. But it wasn't always so bloody. The Aztecs loved gold, and they loved candy – we can thank them for both gum and chocolate.

The Incas were building a kingdom, exceptional...

While the Aztecs ruled what is now Mexico, the **Incas** were busy in the Andes mountains, where they built the biggest kingdom in all the Americas. Based in **Cuzco, Peru**, the Incan empire, at its height in the 12th century, reigned over a territory spanning modern Ecuador to northern Chile. More than a million people lived in its bounds. And there were supposedly close to 20,000 miles of roads connecting the various tribes who lived under the rule of the Incan king.

They built aqueducts in the Andes...

Incan engineers were as sophisticated as any at the time, building acres of farmland on terraces in the Andes. They constructed forts that still stand today – even though they used no mortar between the blocks. They put up aqueducts, and had some of the best medical techniques of the ancient world.

Machu Picchu – the city of the clouds...

Machu Picchu is an extraordinary place for many reasons. It's an ancient city on a 9,000-foot mountaintop with stunning views, but beyond its obvious beauty, it's fascinating because it cannot be seen from below.

But from the ground, it vanished, The secret, never found by the Spanish...

Historians now think this city from the early 1400s was a secret place. It was home to more than 150 houses and palaces, temples, and baths – all up in the clouds. The buildings were carved out of the granite from the mountain. No one knows for sure what the Incas did there, but it was almost certainly used as an astronomic observatory. The Spanish never found Machu Picchu.

Human Sacrifice

An Aztec Mask

HISTORY SPEAKS

"We are not myths of the past, ruins in the jungle or zoos. We are people and we want to be respected, not to be victims of intolerance and racism."

— Rigoberta Menchú, a Maya, 1992

CHAPTER 18:

YOU NEED A RENAISSANCE

The Renaissance, Reformation and Scientific Revolution:
1350 to 1700

INTRO

The **Renaissance** took place in Europe in the 14th and 15th centuries. Historians consider it a renaissance, or rebirth, because it was a time period of unprecedented growth in the arts and sciences, like a revival of the high culture of the Greeks and Romans. This explosion of cultural development followed what had been a rather dark period during the Middle Ages. This was the time of Shakespeare's plays, Galileo's experiments, Michelangelo's paintings, and Martin Luther's new church. A lot was going on.

The Mona Lisa

YOU NEED A RENAISSANCE

LYRICS

Yeah, it's the Renaissance.

There's so little art in the Dark Age,
Just a couple jokers
Like in a card game.
But things change
And those hard days
Turn into the Renaissance,
Now art pays.
Let's get classical,
Take it back to Greeks,
We're smarter now;
We're practically geeks.
The Medici family will pay you
Mad doubloons,
If you paint something
That doesn't look like a cartoon.

So we add perspective,
Paint in 3-D,
Make the background small;
It's easy.
Raphael, Michelangelo,
Leonardo da Vinci, and Donatello.
Aren't those the Ninja Turtles?
Yeah, that's it,
But the Sistine Chapel didn't
Paint itself, kid.
Mona Lisa smiles, that's so new,
Sculpt Greek and Bible dudes in
Their birthday suits.

If you're sick of eating the same
Thing for lunch, stand up!
Nobody's thinking 'cause it's cool
To be dumb, stand up!
There's no art, just guns and greed,
Stand up!

CONTEXT AND BACKGROUND

There's so little art in the Dark Age...

Part of the impetus for the Renaissance was the Black Death, or **bubonic plague,** which killed millions of Europeans. This had one positive effect — it left more in terms of food, resources, and wealth for those who survived. This bounty helped usher in an economic boom. Trade rebounded, a large middle class grew, governments reorganized and life was generally more stable and prosperous. And all of this activity encouraged artists and thinkers to do their thing.

Let's get classical, take it back to Greeks...

The word *renaissance* means "rebirth," and what was reborn was the artistic and philosophical achievements of ancient Greece and Rome. A new breed of mostly Italian artists were extremely interested in the sculpture, paintings, architecture and philosophy of the ancient Greeks and Romans who, they thought, had done things really well.

We're smarter now; we're practically geeks...

These new thinkers went nuts for Greek and Roman writing. They read it, copied and translated it and wrote responses. Most of them wrote with pens, which they had to dip into ink every few seconds. But in Germany, a man named **Johann Gutenberg** (1398-1468) soon changed the world with his invention – a movable-type **printing press**. That is, letters could be rearranged so that multiple books could be printed on the same machine. This forever changed the world of literature, creating an explosion of books.

Prior to Gutenberg's press, there were few copies of titles because it was difficult to make them. With movable type, books could be printed one after the other. Scientists could now share their work easily, for example, and priceless old texts could be preserved for the future. Playwrights like Shakespeare could expose their masterpieces to wide audiences. All of the ideas bubbling about during the Renaissance could be given wide distribution. It was certainly revolutionary.

The Medici Family will pay you mad doubloons...

Great art basically takes two things: amazing artists and people willing to pay the artists (so they don't have to spend all their time farming or fixing toilets or whatever). Lucky for us, the Italian Renaissance had both.

In the 1300s, Italy was a land of city-states. Places like Milan, Venice and Florence were important centers of trade and commerce. No single monarchy ruled in Italy, so powerful families were able to control regions. This was what happened in **Florence**, where the **Medici family** came to power. First, Cosimo de Medici took over the government of the city; then his son Lorenzo followed his father's footsteps. Florence, which had been promoted as a center of intellectual activity under previous rulers, attracted many great minds. The Medici family continued to encourage artists and thinkers, and they became great patrons of culture – they'd pay top dollar to the best artists.

So we add perspective, paint in 3-D...

One of the most impressive innovations of Renaissance painters was thinking about **three dimensions**. To make their paintings more lifelike, artists like Leonardo da Vinci studied how things in the background look smaller. The effect was incredible: Giant canvases or murals showed Greek gods moving among crumbling ruins with ships in the distance; vivid portraits depicted children playing in the background. These little touches added a lot.

Raphael...

For **Raphael Sanzio** (1483-1520), talent was in the blood. The painter's father was also an artist, and Raphael learned a lot about shade and light, depth and perspective from him and others. By the time he was 21 he had painted his first masterpiece, *The Marriage of the Virgin*. When he was ready to head out on his own, Raphael went where the action was — Florence, where he met Michelangelo, Leonardo, and others, and studied their techniques. He was commissioned by the Vatican to do a series of paintings. One of these, *The School of Athens*, is probably his most famous work.

Michelangelo...

One of the beneficiaries of the Medicis was a sculptor named **Michelangelo Buonarroti** (1475-1564). Michelangelo was friendly with Lorenzo de Medici and studied sculpture at his home. The young artist would take what he learned and turn it into masterworks like *David* and the *Pieta*, pieces that remain among the most famous sculptures of all time. Not long after completing them, Michelangelo was hired to paint frescoes on the ceiling of

LYRICS continued

You need a renaissance, stand up!

Do you believe in magic
Like people used to?
You get sick, and you think
God hates you.
They didn't question
What the priests told 'em,
Until a couple of scientists
Got emboldened.
They said, "I won't take your word
As the truth,
If you want me to believe,
You better show me proof."
Poof!
This was the Scientific Revolution,
How you like them apples?
Like Isaac Newton.

Now everybody thought,
God made the Earth,
And put it in the
Center of the universe.
Copernicus thought
It was the sun at center,
Like the gum's at the center of a...
A Blow Pop.
Galileo's telescope
Proved the Earth moved,
The Pope said, "Galileo is a fool."
Actually, the Pope couldn't
Handle the facts,
'Cause science kind of gave him
Like a panic attack.

HOOK

"Tell me, have you sinned?"
Yeah, like every day,
"Well if you pay me lots of money,
I can make it go away."

the **Sistine Chapel** in Rome.

Leonardo da Vinci...
When we use the term Renaissance
Man, we're describing someone like
Leonardo da Vinci (1452-1519). Not
just because he lived during this time
period, but because he was great at
many things. Most famous as the artist
who painted the **Mona Lisa**, Leonardo
was good at most everything he did.
He was a scientist, an inventor – he
could even sing! He painted and
worked on all kinds of scholarly studies,
from geometry to flying machines to
architecture. But he was still able to
come up with some of the world's
most famous paintings, including
The Last Supper and the Mona Lisa.
Unquestionably, the man was a genius.

Donatello...
Like Michelangelo, **Donatello** (1386-
1466) was a sculptor. He was one
of the greatest of all time, and he
made his early mark in Florence,
where he was born in the city. And like
Michelangelo, one of his most famous
pieces was a sculpture called David
– it was the first nude sculpture to be
done in the Renaissance. Donatello
did work for the Medici family,
and his art – which included other
masterpieces like St. George and the
Dragon, St. Mark, St. Peter and St. John
the Evangelist – played with classical
Greek and Roman themes and as well
as Christian ones.

*Do you believe in magic like people
used to...*
The Middle Ages in Europe was a
superstitious time. Few were educated
except for members of the clergy
(priests and monks). To most people,
God worked in mysterious ways, and

129

if it wasn't God, it might be a fairy, demon or witch that made your brother act so strangely. If a town suspected a certain woman was a witch, they might take her from her house, tie her to a stake, and burn her.

You get sick, and you think that God hates you...

The **Spanish Inquisition** was a dark spot during the glory days of the Renaissance. Ferdinand and Isabella, monarchs of Spain, wanted to use religion to unite the Kingdom of Spain under their rule. It had previously been divided up by differing religious factions – Catholics, Protestants, Jews and Muslims. Ferdinand and Isabella thought they could unite the nation if everyone were Catholic. So in 1478 they basically told those who didn't share their beliefs – the so-called "heretics" – to leave. If they didn't leave, members of the Inquisition would arrest, torture and kill them. Thousands were executed. For years, the Inquisition tried to stomp people out simply because they were different.

If you want me to believe you better show me proof...

An amazing revolution occured alongside the artistic changes of the Renaissance. Most people call it the **Scientific Revolution**, but you could call it the "why revolution." Just like an annoying three-year-old, scientists began asking "Why?" to everything. The sky is blue. Why? Some stars don't move straight across the sky; they make circles. Why? These scientists realized that just because their moms and dads told them something was true didn't mean actually it was. They wanted to *observe* the truth.

Poof! This was the Scientific Revolution...

Thanks to the Scientific Revolution, we prove things as either true or false. But how do we go about proving something? To help people, **Francis Bacon** (1561-1626) came up with what is known as the **scientific method**, the idea that a scientific project should begin by observing or exploring an idea or phenomenon. Then the scientist should make his or her theory about how something works – called the hypothesis. After that, the theory should be tested. This is still the way scientists approach their work today.

How you like them apples? Like Isaac Newton...

There is a popular myth that **Isaac Newton** was chilling under an apple tree when an apple fell on his head and this made him "discover" gravity. Erase that image from your mind. There was no apple tree and gravity had already been "discovered." What Newton *did* discover was how all objects pull on each other, and that how much they pull depends on their mass. Newton's theories beefed up the theories of other great scientists, including Copernicus and Galileo.

Copernicus thought it was the sun at center...

Nicolaus Copernicus (1473-1543) was a real troublemaker – according to the Catholic Church, at least. The great Polish astronomer had this idea that the Earth rotated and revolved around the sun. Until that time, everyone believed that the Earth was the center of the universe and the sun rotated around it. Copernicus's ideas got him all kinds of angry mail and the Church banned his landmark book,

LYRICS continued

That's what Catholics did,
Selling indulgences,
Till a monk named Martin Luther
Wasn't feeling it.
Wrote 95 theses and
Tacked 'em up,
Said the Church is too fat
Like a Reese's Cup.
We need to be more
Personal with Jesus,
His friends protested,
So they're Protestants.

Over in England, we find Henry VIII,
With like 30 ladies
That he wanted to date.
Now, you know how dads
Want to play ball with their son?
Well, his wife Catherine
Wasn't giving him one.
So Henry asked the Pope,
"Yo, can I get a divorce?"
But the Pope said, "No, you've
Got to stay the course."
What do you do if you're a king
And your church says wait?
Well, you start your own church
If you're Henry VIII.

Hook

The Revolution of the Holy Spheres.
Scientists now believe that the universe doesn't even have a center.

Galileo's telescope proved the Earth moved...

Another hugely important scientist, **Galileo Galilei** (1564-1642), was one of the few people who thought Copernicus had the right idea. And Galileo could prove it. He invented a **telescope** and looked into space in a way that no one had before. He was then able to see what was orbiting what. His contributions to physics were likewise extraordinary. One of them, still taught in classrooms everywhere, was that the weight of an object doesn't determine how fast it falls. If you drop a heavy item, such as a stone, and a lighter item, like a pin, at the same time, they'll hit the ground at the simultaneously. His findings would change science. For his contributions, the Catholic Church put Galileo under house arrest and made him publicly deny what he had written.

That's what the Catholics did, selling indulgences...

It was time for the Catholic Church, such a powerful force in the Middle Ages, to change. One of the most unpopular practices of the Church was the **selling of indulgences**. Priests said that the more money you gave them for these "indulgences," the faster you'd get into heaven when you died.

Till a monk named Martin Luther wasn't feeling it...

A German monk named **Martin Luther** was outraged by this; to him, it seemed to go against the teachings of Jesus. So, piping mad, Luther scribbled 95 things he hated about the Church on a piece of paper one night, marched down to his church, and tacked them to the door. They were soon known as the **95 Theses** (a thesis is an argument). This was Halloween, 1517. Boo!

Wrote 95 theses and tacked 'em up...

Luther also thought that mass (Catholic church service) should be conducted in the native tongue of the people, not in Latin, which many people didn't understand. His push for change gave birth to the **Reformation**. His followers felt the same way; they wanted to protest against the Church, so they became known as **Protestants**. Nowadays, there are lots of sects that are considered Protestant: Baptists, Anglicans, Lutherans, born- again Christians and many others all trace their origin back to Martin Luther.

Said the church is too fat like a Reese's Cup...

The Reformation hit the Catholic Church hard. All of its major figures – the Pope, cardinals, archbishops – decided a meeting was necessary. They wanted to come up with a plan to address the points made by the Protestants who had left the Church. Some Catholics wanted to try and bring them back; others just wanted to figure out how to move into the future. They wanted to reconsolidate the power and respect of the Church. Over the course of 18 years, starting in 1545, they met at Trent, a town on the border of Germany and Italy. **The Council of Trent** worked — it established a doctrine that the Catholic Church would live by for years.

We need to be more personal with Jesus...

Pope Leo X was the one who had allowed priests to sell indulgences. He did it to raise money for building awesome churches in Rome, including St. Peter's Basilica. In 1521, Leo threw Martin Luther out of the church (excommunication).

Over in England, we find Henry VIII...

When **King Henry VIII** took the throne of England upon the death of his father, people everywhere hailed the new king. He was a scholar, musician and athlete, and his subjects liked him. The new king didn't have much interest in the affairs of the state; he left much of the political work of the time to his aid, Cardinal Thomas Wolsey. Some scholars claim Wolsey was the real power behind the throne. Henry was famous for many things – he had six wives, several of whom ended up imprisoned in the famous Tower of London. (They are said to haunt the place.) He was opposed to Luther and his reforms, and for that Pope Leo X gave him the title "Defender of the Faith." But he later declared himself the supreme head of the Church of England, effectively breaking ties with Rome.

You know how dads want to play ball with their son...

It all began when Henry was married to his first wife, **Catherine of Aragon**. They had a girl together, "Bloody Mary" (see below), but no boys. That bothered old Henry; he really wanted a son to be the next king. Plus, he was kind of eyeing this lady-in-waiting at the court named **Anne Boleyn**. So he asked Pope Clement for a divorce. The Catholic Church forbade divorce, but Clement had personal reasons for saying no as well. Henry basically replied, "Fine, if you won't let me get divorced, I'll start my own church and I'll grant myself a divorce." He did, and the church he founded is known as the Anglican Church or the Church of England.

Well, his wife Catherine wasn't giving him one...

Queen Mary I will always be known by her nickname — Bloody Mary. Mary only reigned for five years, but during that time she had a lot of people killed, hence the name. One of the first things she did when she took office was have her cousin and potential rival, Jane Grey, killed. Mary was intent upon returning England to the Roman Catholic Church, so she decided that the Protestants that had been growing in numbers in England would simply have to be put to death. Hundreds of Protestant leaders were executed during her reign. She married Phillip II, King of Spain, who ruled during the Spanish Inquisition.

Well, you start your own church if you're Henry VIII...

Next upon the English throne was Mary's half-sister, **Elizabeth I**. She had been imprisoned by Queen Mary in the Tower of London, a landmark structure known for its many famous prisoners. When she took the throne in 1559, Elizabeth set about undoing much of Mary's work. Many consider her one of the greatest monarchs in English history. She established the Church of England once and for all. During her reign the English defeated the Spanish Armada and became a major power player in European politics. And during the **Elizabethan Age**, the arts flourished

in England.

Many scholars give the title of "most important writer ever" to Elizabethan poet and playwright **William Shakespeare** (1564-1616). And it's hard to argue with this claim since his work has been read and his plays performed almost constantly since his day. He wrote 37 plays – *Hamlet, Romeo and Juliet, Othello,* and *Macbeth* among them. During his lifetime, his plays were performed at the Globe Theatre. It was a famous playhouse in London that seated 3,000 and was affordable for most people. One of the biggest and most influential people in all of academia, he never attended college. It would be virtually impossible to list the number of references to Shakespeare's work in our cultural history since his death.

Henry VIII

CHAPTER 19:

MAJOR WORLD RELIGIONS
Bonus
5000 BC to Today

INTRO

Religion may be as old as language, or even older. It developed from a fundamental human quality: to ask questions and try to answer them. Why is there day and night? What is the sun? Why do humans exist? Different religions all sought to answer these questions and many others. Some of them have, over time, been answered by science, but religion still serves an important role in many people's lives. Some of the enduring qualities of most religions is that they offer meaning and comfort, and teach us lessons about how to live.

God, as Drawn by Michelangelo

MAJOR WORLD RELIGIONS

LYRICS

Judaism:
The Jewish faith began
With Abraham,
Who led the Hebrew people
To the Promised Land.
Hebrews, also known as Jews,
Were unusual at this time.
There was only one god,
And they didn't paint his picture,
They didn't believe
He had a little sister.
Their god was a jealous god;
That's what he said,
So don't pray to false idols,
It'll make him mad.
Moses came down
With ten suggestions,
I mean, Ten Commandments
To command 'em.
To honor thy mother and father,
Don't steal or kill,
And every week,
Take a day off and just chill.

Christianity:
Our religion is monotheistic,
To some the start ain't realistic.
We don't understand,
What's the debate, son?
We make a quarter
Of the world's population.
Made a book out of the stories
That we lived then,
Became big enough to make a
State religion.
Jesus was a Jew,
He started something new,
Said, "Do nice to others,

CONTEXT AND BACKGROUND

The Jewish faith began with Abraham...
The **Jewish** faith began with **Abraham**, who led the Hebrew people to the "Promised Land." This was sometime between 2000 and 1500 BC. The Jews (also known as the **Hebrews**) were unusual at the time for believing in only one god. Most everyone else around them worshipped multiple deities. The Jews called their god Yahweh, and he told them in the Ten Commandments to worship only him. So they did. They followed Abraham out of Mesopotamia and followed Moses out of Egypt, because God said so.

Hebrews, also known as Jews...
Canaan was a land on the Mediterranean where Israel is today. It was a very important place to the Jews, who moved there thousands of years ago when they marched from Mesopotamia with Abraham. In about 2000 BC, the Jews migrated to Egypt to find water and work. When they returned to Canaan in 1200 BC, they found...guess what? People had moved in while they were gone. The Jews claimed rights to the land, based on their history there, but the Canaanites didn't want to give it up. So they fought. The land of Israel, claimed by both the Jews (Israelis) and the Palestinians, is still being fought over today.

There was only one god, and they didn't paint his picture...
The second commandment states: "You shall not make for yourself an idol, or any likeness of what is in

heaven above." So, to this day Jews (and Christians and Muslims) do not paint pictures of God or make statues of him. Many other cultures throughout time did pray to images of their gods: the Hindus, Egyptians, Greeks, Romans, the Norse, Aztec and more.

Their god was a jealous god; that's what he said...

The second commandment also states: "You shall not worship them or serve [other gods]; for I, the Lord your god, am a jealous god, and I will send punishment on the children for the wrongdoing of their fathers, to the third and fourth generation of those who hate me; and I will have mercy through a thousand generations on those who have love for me and keep my laws."

Moses came down with ten suggestions. I mean Ten Commandments...

Like Abraham, **Moses** was a prophet who spoke to God. He was famous for a few things. First, he led the Jews out of Egypt, where they'd gone to escape drought or famine in Canaan. For a time the Jews lived a nice life in the land of the pharaohs, but soon their growing numbers concerned for the pharaoh, who thought they were getting too powerful. So he had them all enslaved. It was Moses who got them out of this bad situation. Known as the Exodus, this was a turning point in Judaism. Moses was also the man to whom God gave the Ten Commandments, according to the Judaeo-Christian story.

To honor thy mother and father, don't steal or kill...

The Jewish faith is based largely on five books; add them up and you have the **Torah**, also known as the Five Books of Moses. This sacred Hebrew text comes on large scrolls made from kosher animal parchment. The Jews believe it contains information that came from God to Moses. It features both a history of the Hebrew people and 613 laws. The Jews consider the Torah so sacred, they don't even touch it. It's read with a pointer. Also made up of five parts, the Torah is just one of three texts that comprise the Hebrew Bible.

And every week, take a day off and just chill...

Since Jesus was a Jew, Christians didn't write a brand-new bible for themselves; they just added to the Jewish Bible. So the **Ten Commandments** are the same in both the Jewish and Christian religions. Both faiths believe they were the 10 laws that God gave to Moses on Mount Sinai to bring back to the people. They form the basis of law in many countries. And, because Moses was a major prophet to Muslims, they are referred to in Islam as well.

We don't understand, what's the debate, son...

The Christians had it rough in the early days of their religion. They were Roman subjects and the Romans worshipped multiple gods. When the city of Rome had a huge fire during Nero's regime, he blamed the fire on the Christians, and they were persecuted. Over time, though, Jesus's disciples began to spread their new religion. Unlike the Jews, who hardly ever converted new followers, Christians actively recruited new members. Christianity became a much larger force under the Roman emperor **Constantine**, who converted

LYRICS continued

They'll do nice to you."
But father, please forgive them,
You know this world is filled with sin.
We believe that he died
And he came back,
But others just couldn't
Understand that.
Disciples believed that
The Trinity's the one,
That's why we pray in the name of
The father and the son, son.
And the Holy Ghost, ya dig?

Thou shall not kill.
Turn the other cheek.
Avoid extremes,
Find the middle way.
Fixed in yoga, do thy work.
There is no God but Allah, and
Muhammad is his prophet.

Islam:
Now, the same angel
Who showed up to Mary,
To tell her she was going to give
Birth to God's kid,
This angel appeared
To Muhammad, told him he was
Going to be the next prophet.
Now he's Islamic,
And he founded Islam,
And he wrote a holy book,
That's the holy Qur'an.
Called God Allah;
That means one true good,
Laid down five pillars
And here they are.
One, there's no god but God,
I testify.
Two, every day you've
Gotta pray five times.

to Christianity and pushed the faith all across his empire.

We make a quarter of the world's population…

Christianity grew quickly, mostly within Europe, though it would spread across the globe. A 2005 survey found that Christianity is the most practiced religion on Earth (33% of the world's population), followed by Islam (20%); Hinduism (13%); Chinese folk religions including Confucianism, Taoism and Shintoism (6%); and Buddhism (6%). Judaism has remained a small religion (0.23%), but essentially gave birth to both Christianity and Islam.

Made a book out the story that we live then…

The **Bible** of Christianity comes in two parts — the **Old Testament** and the **New Testament**. The Old Testament is nearly the same as the Hebrew Bible; it tells the history of the Jews. The New Testament tells the story of Jesus, his life on Earth, his death, and what Christians believe happened thereafter. Some Christians take the Bible's text literally, while others see its stories and lessons as a guide.

Became big enough to make a state religion…

By 380 Christianity had become the official state religion of the Roman Empire, and it would serve as the official religion of many European nations up to the present day. Islam is currently the official religion of many states in the Middle East. America, in contrast, has no official religion – the Founding Fathers wanted to be very clear about that. As George Washington and John Adams wrote, "The government of the United

FLOCAB SPITS FACTS LIKE AN ALMANAC

The 10 Commandments in Brief

1. I am God, one and only

2. Don't make pictures of anything in heaven

3. Don't use my name in vain

4. Rest one day per week

5. Honor you mom and dad

6. Don't kill

7. Don't cheat on your spouse

8. Don't steal

9. Don't lie

10. Don't desire your neighbor's stuff

States of America is not, in any sense, founded on the Christian religion."

Jesus was a Jew, he started something new...
There is little doubt that Jesus was a real, historical figure. He was a Jew who was angered by the hypocrisy he saw around him. He was upset that people followed the laws of the Torah without spiritually connecting with God, and he didn't think they did enough to help those who were sick and poor. In his lifetime, he attracted quite a following. These people weren't called Christians; they were just Jews who liked what Jesus had to say.

Said "Do nice to others, they'll do nice to you"...
One of Jesus's most famous speeches is called the **Sermon on the Mount**. In this amazing sermon, Jesus dropped his **"golden rule"** ("Do unto others what you would have them do to you"); told people to "turn the other cheek"; noted that the meek will inherit the Earth; and instructed people not to judge "lest you be judged" as well. Many people say this sermon contained the founding principles of Christianity.

But father, please forgive them, you know this world is full of sin...
Eventually, Jesus attracted a large group of followers who called him a **messiah**, a savior or liberator of the Jewish people. This caught the attention of both the local priests and the Roman authorities, who thought he might start an open rebellion. So they tried him in court as an enemy of the state. Jesus was found guilty and crucified, the typical way that Romans

LYRICS continued

Three, if people don't have money,
Give them some.
Four, better fast during Ramadan.
Five, if your mommy and your
Daddy let ya,
Make the holy pilgrimage
Over to Mecca.
After Muhammad died,
Two groups started to fight,
That's the Sunnis and the Shiite,
Alright?

Hinduism:
They say,
I'm the body of philosophies,
Barely understood,
But I crossed the seas.
India, 1500 BC,
Other thoughts came together
With me.
Reincarnation,
That's when you come back,
Depending on your karma,
How you interact.
So stay calm and do your yoga,
I'll bring you wisdom; I'm Hinduism.

Buddhism:
Buddha, my name,
The awakened one,
Embrace the pain,
It all became one.
Follow me,
I bring thought elevation,
Then bring you closer
Through meditation.
And I'm life,
So with words I'll trade you,
I'm so popular, all through Asia.
India, China, then Malaysia,
I'll amaze you, like Ali and Frazier.

put people to death.

We believe that he died and he came back...
According to the Christian Bible, three days after he died, Jesus was resurrected, or brought back to life. In the following days, he appeared to various people and, apparently, told the **apostles** (his close followers and students) to spread his teachings throughout the world (up to that point, Jesus had directed his teachings to other Jews). Jesus also promised to come to Earth again to resurrect the dead and judge everyone.

Christians believe that Jesus died for all humanity's sins. To most Christians, the way to heaven is to accept that Jesus made this powerful sacrifice.

Disciples believe the Trinity's one...
Jesus himself didn't speak directly about the **Trinity**; instead it was created during a pow-wow between top Catholic officials hundreds of years after his death. These priests got together at **Nicaea** to discuss some important questions: Is Jesus a god? Was he human? If he is part-god, does that make Christianity a polytheistic faith? The Church elders decided to compromise: Jesus is 100% god and 100% human. Jesus (the son), God (the father), and something called the Holy Spirit are all God, but God is only one. This is the Trinity. During the Inquisition, famous people who disagreed with this theory were tortured during the Inquisition.

This angel appeared to Muhammad, told him he was going to be the next prophet...
Another powerful prophet,

Muhammad, is the man who begot the Muslim faith. He was born in **Mecca** in 570 AD. According to Islam, the angel Gabriel appeared to him when he was 40, bringing the message of God. For the next 23 years, the angel visited Muhammad on many occasions, each time giving him new messages from God. These were written down into the **Qur'an.** Like Jesus, Muhammad's role was to teach the people, and demonstrate the correct way to behave.

Now he's Islamic, and he founded Islam...

The **Islamic faith,** the religion of Muslims, dates back to the time just after Muhammad's death, around 650 AD. Muslims believe that Moses and Jesus were prophets, but that Muhammad was the last prophet. Their bible, the Qur'an, includes many of the same stories as the Old Testament, which is part of the Jewish and Christian faiths. So there are more similarities than not between the three religions.

The Islamic faith followed the prophet Muhammad very closely. Through him, Allah gave the Muslims the Five Pillars, and told them not to eat pork or drink alcohol.

Called God Allah; that means one true god...

Allah is the Arabic word for God, literally meaning "the one god." Some Westerners believe that the Muslim god is named Allah (like the Greek's most important god was named Zeus), as opposed to the Christian god, whose name, it seems, is just "God." But this is wrong. Arabic Christians and Jews call their god "Allah" as well. And since Islam is a continuation of the faith started by Abraham (just like Judaism and Christianity), it's clear that Allah and God are the same. This makes it even more heartbreaking to see members of the various religions kill each other over religious differences.

Laid down five pillars and here they are...

The **Five Pillars of Islam** are somewhat similar to the Ten Commandments – they are supposed to be laws straight from the mouth of God, telling you how you should behave. In fact, the first of the Five Pillars is the same as the first of the Ten Commandments: Allah wants you to have no other god but Allah. In other words, believe only in me. The other four instruct Muslims to pray to God five times a day, facing toward the holy land of Mecca; to make a pilgrimage to Mecca someday; to be charitable toward the poor; and to fast during Ramadan, the holy month.

Four, better fast during Ramadan...

Ramadan happens during the ninth month of the Muslim calendar. It often occurs in September but is dependent upon the cycles of the moon. During this sacred time, Muslims fast from sunrise to sundown. They eat a very small meal before dawn breaks and another small meal after dark. They devote extra time on their prayers and with their family, and practice a sort of ritual cleansing that includes things like: not gossiping, not touching things that belong to others, not saying or listening to bad words, and not going to bad places.

Make the holy pilgrimage over to Mecca...

Mecca is a city in Saudi Arabia. More

important to Muslims, it's the birthplace of the prophet Muhammad. Inside the Great Mosque at Mecca is the Kaaba, a rectangular building that is the most holy place for Muslims. They believe the prophet Abraham built it, and it's what they face toward during their daily ritual prayers. Even before Muhammad, it was considered an important, sacred city. The second holiest city after Mecca is Medina, the place where Muhammad was buried.

A visit to the holy city of Mecca is something every Muslim is supposed to do at some point during their lives. This religious journey is called a pilgrimage. Pilgrimages are common to many religions but are especially important to Islam.

That's the Sunnis and the Shiite, alright...
After Muhammad died, the Islamic faith split into two branches — Sunni and Shiite (or Shi'ah). The **Sunnis** believe that the first four caliphs, or heirs to Muhammad, were the rightful successors to the prophet. Their descendants ruled the Arab world to after World War I. The **Shiites** think that only one of those caliphs, Ali, was legitimate, and that only his sons, or heirs, should rule. Those sons disappeared in 931, so the Shiites believe that for a long time there was no one who had the divine right to lead them. The two groups often fight to this day.

They say, I'm the body of philosophies...
Hinduism is a truly unique religion in that it had no founder. It just sort of developed, along with the culture and religious traditions of India. Unlike other religions it doesn't have a single dogma – a system of beliefs – but many. It has numerous subsets, and people who practice Hinduism can have very different ideas or interpretations from each other.

Barely understood, but I crossed the seas...
Because Hinduism is so diverse, some of its followers believe in multiple gods; others believe in only one; some believe in none. Nearly all believe that the soul is eternal, and that a life force, Brahma, exists throughout everything.

India, 1500 BC...
Hinduism is one of the oldest of the still-practiced religions of the world. It came to India with the Aryans (c. 1500 BC) and merged and morphed with the other religions of the time.

Reincarnation, that's when you come back...
One of the traditions that developed in Hinduism is **reincarnation** — the idea that our souls migrate to a new body upon death. According to Hinduism, what we come back as depends on our **karma**, the good or bad actions we commit in our lifetime.

So stay calm and do your yoga...
Hinduism also stresses **meditation**. To meditate is to get in touch with Brahma, the universal life force, by relaxing and focusing only on your breath. Meditation is related to yoga, a system of stretching and body movements that have been practiced in some form for thousands of years.

Buddha, my name...
Imagine walking away from everything you ever had into an uncertain future – and you're a rich and privileged

141

person. That's what **Siddhartha Guatama** did in about 528 BC. In India, he left his cushy role as prince to wander the countryside looking for life's answers. It worked out well for him – if you believe the stories of Buddhism. Unhappy with the Hindu religion, Siddhartha traveled around and meditated for quite some time, trying to understand why pain exists. Then he found what he was looking for — enlightenment. From then on he was known as the **Buddha,** or "enlightened one."

Follow me, I bring thought elevation...
Buddhism spread all across India. People liked it as an alternative to Hinduism. It was a simple, peaceful, loving faith, and when people heard about its tenets in other parts of Asia, they took to them as well. Soon Buddhism would be one of the largest religions in the world, spreading throughout India and China, two of the planet's most populous places. People in India liked that Buddhism broke with the caste system, and that it called for an end to human suffering.

What are the other major world religions?

Other popular religions and philosophies thrive in Asia. Confucianism is popular in China, while Shinto was once the state religion of Japan.

At roughly the same time the Buddha was wandering around India, **Confucius** (551-479 BC) was teaching in China. Some people confuse his philosophies with religion, but they were more ways of thinking and behaving than a spiritual set of beliefs. Born into poverty, Confucius somehow educated himself to the fullest to

become the most important thinker in Chinese history. His ideas about virtue, family, and society became the foundation for the moral code of China. He thought that children should respect their parents, citizens should obey their government and people should adhere to high standards of behavior if they expect others to.

Buddhism is often mixed with **Shinto** in Japan; in fact, most people there practice both. Shinto is another ancient religion, dating back to about 500 BC. It's unusual, like Hinduism, because it has no real founder and its church structure or organizing body is not rigid. Shinto is also unlike other major religions in that it doesn't have a written scripture or body of laws that its practitioners are supposed to adhere to. It's based on the idea of **kami,** or the Shinto deities. But they're not gods like the omnipotent gods of other religions; they are more like spirit forces that look after humans and help them. And they're often found in natural objects or creatures and in special people. There are four affirmations in Shinto: honor of tradition and family; love of nature; physical cleanliness; and matsuri, the worship of kami. People who believe in Shinto often incorporate other ideas into their religion, like Taoism, Confucianism, and, as mentioned earlier, Buddhism.

HISTORY SPEAKS

"All religions, arts and sciences are branches of the same tree. All these aspirations are directed toward ennobling man's life, lifting it from the sphere of mere physical existence and leading the individual toward freedom."

– Albert Einstein

"When I do good, I feel good; when I do bad, I feel bad. That's my religion."

– Abraham Lincoln

Music Credits

1. We're Nomadic
Lyrics: Harrison
Music: Boyer
Vocals: Escher, Trajik, Rappaport

2. We're in that Fertile Crescent
Lyrics: Harrison
Music: Shadowville Productions
Vocals: Escher, Trajik

3. Hammurabi's Code & Twelve Tables of Rome (Interlude)
Music: Rappaport
Vocals: Reason, Rappaport

4. Walk Like an Egyptian
Lyrics: Harrison
Music: XO Music
Vocals: Escher, Grey, Netty

5. It Goes Round and Round
Lyrics: Harrison
Music: Boyer
Vocals: Escher, Rappaport

6. Chinese Knowledge
Lyrics: Harrison
Music: Rappaport
Vocals: Grey

7. Art of War & Legalism (Interlude)
Music: Ed Boyer
Vocals: Dillon, Escher

8. Like a Persian
Lyrics: Baba Brinkman
Music: Ed Boyer
Vocals: Escher

9. Party at the Parthenon
Lyrics: Dillon
Music: Batsauce
Vocals: Dillon

10. I am Spartacus
Lyrics: Harrison
Music: Ed Boyer
Vocals: Escher

11. Gettin' Byzzy with It
Lyrics: Harrison
Music: Rappaport
Vocals: Trajik, Escher

12. Middle Ages: Europe
Lyrics: Spectac, Harrison
Music: Rappaport
Vocals: Spectac, Escher

Music Credits

13. Middle Ages: Asia
Lyrics: J Bully, Harrison
Music: Boyer
Vocals: J Bully, Escher

14. Middle Ages: Africa
Lyrics: Harrison, Spectac
Music: Boyer
Vocals: Escher, Spectac, J Bully

15. African Proverbs (Interlude)
Music: Rappaport
Vocals: Escher, Netty

16. Empires of Islam
Lyrics: Harrison, Reason
Music: Boyer
Vocals: Escher, Reason

17. Hay Nativos
Lyrics: Dillon, Harrison
Music: Batsauce
Vocals: Dillon, Escher, Ben Hameen

18. You Need a Renaissance
Lyrics: Harrison
Music: Sean Devine
Vocals: Escher, Netty, Trajik

19. World Religions (Bonus)
Lyrics: Escher, Trajik
Music: Boyer
Vocals: Escher, Trajik

All music recorded at Flocabulary
Studios, New York, NY; The Sweatshop
Studio, Atlanta, GA; and NCCU
Studios, Durham, NC
Music production by Alex Rappaport
and Dillon Maurer
Engineered by Alex Rappaport
Mixed by Alex Rappaport and Dillon
Maurer
Mastered by Music House Mastering
Published by Escher Robinson Music
(ASCAP)

Photo & Illustration Credits

Photo & Illustration Credits

Georgia); Made in Constantinople

Chapter 12, page 86—*Codex Manesse 081* by Walther von Klingen

page 89—*Ghent Altarpiece* by Jan van Eyck painting, 1432.

Chapter 13, page 92, 99—*Portrait of Yoritomo* by Fujiwara No Takanobu.

page 94—*Early Japanese Images* by Terry Bennett. (Rutland, Vermont: Charles E. Tuttle Company, 1996), 75, 139, pl. 35

page 97, *Mongol Soldiers* by Rashid al-Din, 1305.

Chapter 14, page 100—*Great Mosque of Djenné* by Andy Gilham, 2003.

page 102—*Mansa Musa* by Abraham Cresques of Mallorca, 1375.

page 104-5—*Three Camels* by Jordan Busson, 2008.

Chapter 15, page 106—*Griot in Niger* by Rolland, 2006.

Chapter 16, page 110--*Taj Mahal* by Amal Mongia, 2007.

page 112—*The Prayer at the Tomb'* by Ludwig Deutsch, German. Oil, 1898.

page 117—*The Palace Guard* by Ludwig Deutsch, 1892.

Chapter 17, page 122—*Machu Picchu Sunriseachu Picchu Sunrise,* by Allard Smith, 2005.

page 124—*Turquoise Aztec Mask,* photograph by Z-m-k, 2006.

page 125—*Aztec ritual human sacrifice portrayed in Codex Magliabechiano,* 16th Century.

Chapter 18, page 126—*Mona Lisa* by Leonardo da Vinci, 16th Century.

page 133—*Portrait of Henry VII,* by Hans Holbein the Younger.

Chapter 19, page 134—*Creation of the Sun and Moon* by MIchelango, Sistine Chapel, 1508-1512.

Notes: